335

EGYPT

Robert Pateman/Salwa El-Hamamsy

BENCHMARK BOOKS

MARSHALL CAVENDISH
NEW YORK

PICTURE CREDITS
Cover photo: © Art Directors & TRIP/Adina Tovy
ANA: 60, 62 • Giulio Andreini: 46, 49, 90 • APA Photo Agency: 68 • Art Directors & TRIP:
1, 5, 6, 30, 47, 67, 71, 72, 76, 86, 89 • Bes Stock: 9, 18, 94 • British Museum: 93 • Christine
Osborne Pictures: 8, 10, 11, 19, 22, 26, 37, 39, 53, 55, 56, 57, 63, 73, 75, 77, 80, 82, 84, 87,
98, 99, 101, 102, 103, 104, 105 (both), 107, 108, 109, 113, 114, 117, 118, 121, 123, 125, 126,
127, 128 • Embassy of the Arab Republic of Egypt, Singapore: 32 • Focus Team: 44, 50
• HBL Network: 15, 106 • The Image Bank: 3, 7, 16, 17, 20, 21, 23, 24, 34, 41, 43, 61 (both),
81, 92, 95, 100, 129 • Life File Photographic Library: 12, 13 (bottom), 38, 83, 85 • Lonely
Planet Images: 52, 112 • Robert Pateman: 4, 13 (top), 14, 35, 40, 42, 54, 58, 59, 66, 70, 110,
116 • Times Media: 130, 131 • UPI/Bettmann: 29, 31 • Nik Wheeler: 36, 48, 120

ACKNOWLEDGMENTS
With thanks to Jennifer Houser Wegner, Ph.D., Research Scientist, Egyptian Section,
University of Pennsylvania Museum, for her expert reading of this manuscript

PRECEDING PAGE
An Egyptian family take time out for a group hug during their visit to the ancient temples
of Karnak, near the city of Luxor.

Marshall Cavendish Corporation
99 White Plains Road
Tarrytown, NY 10591
Website: www.marshallcavendish.com

Originated and designed by
Times Books International, an imprint of
Times Media Private Limited, a member of
Times International Publishing

Printed in Malaysia

Library of Congress Cataloging-in-Publication Data
Pateman, Robert, 1954-
Egypt / by Robert Pateman, Salwa El-Hamamsy.— 2nd ed.
   p. cm. — (Cultures of the world)
Summary: Explores the geography, history, government, economy, people,
and culture of Egypt.
Includes bibliographical references and index.
   ISBN 0-7614-1670-6
1. Egypt—Juvenile literature. [1. Egypt.] I. El-Hamamsy, Salwa. II.
Title. III. Series.
DT49.P38 2003
962—dc21   2003009859

7 6 5 4 3

CONTENTS

A Bedouin nomad and his camel.

A mosque in Cairo.

INTRODUCTION

FOR MANY CENTURIES, Egypt has played a very influential role in culture, politics, and civilization, both regionally and internationally. Located at the heart of the world map, Egypt has been the subject and source of many cultural developments since the dawn of human civilization. Egypt has often been at the focus of major historical movements in the Middle East.

Through its history, Egypt has undergone significant cultural and social changes brought about by various economic and political factors. Cultural life in present-day Egypt is a blend of different peoples and represents just one link in a long chain of cultures past.

Modern Egyptian culture reflects the peculiarities of a country with a deep-rooted history and a people whose ancestors were among the first human beings to experience culture and civilization.

GEOGRAPHY

EGYPT IS SITUATED in the northeastern corner of the African continent. It is the 12th largest country in Africa, with a land area of 384,345 square miles (995,450 square km), which is about the combined size of Texas and California. Egypt is bordered by Sudan in the south; Libya in the west; the Mediterranean Sea in the north; and Israel, the Gulf of Aqaba, and the Red Sea in the east.

Egypt is largely desert land and receives very little rain. However, the Nile River flows through the country, watering a fertile green valley. North of Cairo, the river widens to form the Nile delta. Ninety-eight percent of Egypt's population live in the valley and delta of the Nile.

West of the Nile is the Libyan, or Western, Desert, with its oases; to the east lies the more mountainous and barren Arabian, or Eastern, Desert.

Left: **The Rosetta channel on the western Nile delta.**

Opposite: **The bust of the mysterious sphinx looks over the Giza plateau. Much of the original detail of the rock sculpture has been destroyed through centuries of erosion by the natural elements of the desert environment.**

GEOGRAPHIC REGIONS

Egypt can be divided into four main geographic regions: the Nile valley and delta, the Western Desert, the Eastern Desert, and the Sinai Peninsula.

NILE VALLEY AND DELTA The Nile is the world's longest river. It flows from two lakes south of the equator in eastern Africa northward into countries such as Uganda and Sudan where it leaves tropical Africa and enters desert lands, transforming them with life-giving water. Before emptying into the Mediterranean Sea, the river courses through Egypt, which the Greek historian Herodotus called "the gift of the Nile."

Altogether the Nile is 4,145 miles (6,671 km) long, a little longer than the Amazon river in Brazil. Some 1,000 miles (1,609 km) of the Nile run through Egypt. The Egyptians have settled the river's thin green fertile valley that extends the length of the country. This valley is usually about 6 miles (9.7 km) wide, but is narrower in some places. In the past, the African rainy season would increase the amount of water flowing into the Nile and produce annual floods. The Aswan High Dam, however, changed this ancient pattern; the last flood occurred in the mid-1960s.

Upon reaching the delta, the Nile splits into hundreds of branches, creating a fertile fan-shaped area that is 100 miles (161 km) long and 155 miles (249 km) wide by the time the river finally reaches the sea. North of Cairo, the Nile branches into the Damietta and Rosetta channels, both named after the major cities at the end of their course. The delta contains 60 percent of Egypt's useable land though it also has several shallow lakes and swamps that are too salty to be used for cultivation.

Two miles (3.2 km) long and 364 feet (111 m) high, the Aswan High Dam took 10 years to build and resulted in Lake Nasser.

THE EASTERN DESERT The Eastern, or Arabian, Desert stretches east from the Nile River to the Red Sea coast; mountains border the Red Sea. This was once a fertile area, and it still has ancient valleys, or *wadi* (wah-DEE), that were once riverbeds. The desert also has fossilized forests, where the sand is littered with the remains of millions of ancient trees.

It was once thought that human habitation in the Eastern Desert was confined to the coastal areas, but two nomadic peoples have been discovered living in the inner parts of the desert.

There is more activity on the coast, which is an important center for Egypt's oil and tourism industries, with onshore and offshore drilling facilities and resort cities such as Hurghada.

A beach resort at Hurghada.

THE WESTERN DESERT Two-thirds of Egypt's land area is covered by the Western, or Libyan, Desert. Part of the Great Sahara, it stretches across northern Africa from the Atlantic coast all the way to the Nile valley.

Most of the Western Desert consists of a sandy plateau. Close to the border is an area known as the Great Sand Sea, where the sand dunes take the form that most people expect to see in a real desert. The wind controls the shape and movement of the sand dunes. Some dunes may move a few hundred feet a year, while others are almost stationary.

Waterwheels abound in El Faiyûm, the largest oasis town in Egypt.

There are a few mountains in the Western Desert; Jabal Uweinat in the far southwest is the tallest at 6,255 feet (1,907 m). More impressive than the mountains are the great depressions that can drop several hundred feet below sea level. The largest of these is the Qattâra Depression, which at its deepest falls 436 feet (133 m) below sea level. The Qattâra starts just south of the Mediterranean coast and covers 7,000 square miles (18,130 square km).

Few spots in the world are as inhospitable as the heart of the Western Desert, where temperatures can rise as high as 120°F (49°C). Moreover, with no cloud cover to retain the heat, night temperatures tend to be very low, sometimes below freezing. Yet some species of birds, snakes, scorpions, and lizards manage to survive in the Western Desert, except where there are shifting sand dunes.

There are six major oases in the Western Desert. The inhabitants grow palm trees and other crops to support themselves. They also work in factories, packing top-quality dates to be trucked to Cairo.

THE SINAI PENINSULA   The Sinai is a barren desert peninsula. Geographically it is really part of Asia more than of Africa. The Sinai is bordered by three bodies of water: the Gulf of Aqaba in the east, the Gulf of Suez in the west, and the Mediterranean Sea in the north. Since the completion of the Suez Canal, the Sinai has been physically cut off from the rest of Egypt.

In ancient times, the Sinai was a wild and inhospitable desert area that formed a formidable barrier between Egypt and its Middle Eastern neighbors. The ancient Egyptians did little in the region except send the occasional mining expedition in search of turquoise, copper, and other minerals. There were two major turquoise mines in the Sinai that the Egyptians exploited for thousands of years, but the mines no longer produce profitable yields.

The Sinai is flat and sandy in the north. The south is far more mountainous and boasts the highest point in Egypt—Jabal Katrina, or Mount Catherine, at 8,560 feet (2,609 m). Another impressive peak in the area is Jabal Musa, or Mount Sinai, at 7,380 feet (2,249 m).

The Bedouin people have always lived in the Sinai, traditionally as nomads moving from oasis to oasis. In ancient times, the Bedouin were fierce warriors, and the Egyptians only ventured into the Sinai under military protection. Today many Bedouin have abandoned the nomadic way of life and instead make a living from a combination of date farming and raising livestock.

Serrated mountain ridges are a striking feature of the southern Sinai.

THE SUEZ CANAL

The Suez Canal is an artificial waterway that links the Mediterranean Sea with the Red Sea. The canal is 120 miles (193 km) long, 197 feet (60 m) wide, and 66 feet (20 m) deep—big enough to accommodate ships up to 150,000 tons in weight.

The first stretch of the Suez Canal runs from Port Said on the Mediterranean to the city of Isma'iliya on the shores of Lake Timsah. A smaller section of the canal links this lake with the Bitter Lakes. From here a third section continues to Suez and the Red Sea. The canal cuts 6,000 miles (9,656 km) off the sea journey between Europe and Asia, and three convoys make the 15-hour trip through the canal everyday.

The Suez Canal was the brainchild of a Frenchman, Ferdinand de Lesseps. In 1854 he got permission from the *khedive* (kai-DEV), the Turkish governor of Egypt, to start construction. The next year, an International Technical Commission examined the possible routes, and work began in 1859. Ten years later, on November 17, 1869, a fleet of ships assembled at Port Said to make the maiden sailing through the canal. They reached Suez three days later, after being entertained en route at a ball given by the *khedive*. Except between 1967 and 1975, when it was closed as a result of the Arab-Israeli war, the canal has been a very busy waterway and has been enlarged several times to cope with increasing traffic and bigger ships.

CLIMATE

Egypt has a generally hot and arid climate, but there can be a marked difference between winter and summer temperatures. Temperatures in Cairo can rise to 95°F (35°C) in summer and fall to 48°F (9°C) in winter. Farther south, the weather becomes hotter. Winters in Aswân are pleasantly warm, but summer temperatures can reach 104°F (40°C).

Alexandria in the north enjoys milder weather than the rest of the country. The highest temperature Alexandria experiences during the year does not usually rise beyond 86°F (30°C), and the cool Mediterranean breeze makes even the hottest days pleasant.

Egypt gets very little rain. Away from the influence of the Nile, Egypt quickly becomes a desert land. Cairo sees an average of five or fewer

Above and below: **Dates are Egypt's most common fruit.**

rainy days a year, and most of this rain falls between November and January. Siwa, an oasis in the middle of the Western Desert, might get rain only once or twice in a century.

FLORA

Much of Egypt's plant life is found in the Nile valley and delta and in the oases. The date palm, for example, is the most common indigenous tree. It has many uses, and there are at least 30 varieties of date palms in Egypt.

Papyrus, a water reed, is one of the most interesting and useful plants in Egypt. The ancient Egyptians used this plant to make sheets of paper-like material. Today papyrus grows mainly in the south of the country.

Proof of the abundance of plant life in ancient Egypt can be found in the country's fossilized forests, where the remains of trees millions of years old have turned to stone.

There are no forests in Egypt, but there are several common species of trees. Acacia trees grow in many parts, as do carob, eucalyptus, and sycamore trees. There are also cypress, elm, and fruit trees. Many of these trees are not indigenous but were introduced from other countries at different times in the past.

Plants in the desert areas tend to be very specialized in order to survive in the harsh desert environment. Examples of Egyptian desert plants are coarse alfa grass and stunted tamarisks as well as a variety of thorny shrubs and herbs.

FAUNA

The camel is used as a means of transportation and is also a tourist attraction.

Egypt has few large animal species. There was more wildlife in ancient times, and tomb paintings show ostriches, crocodiles, hippopotamuses, and even giraffes. Pressure from the human population has wiped them out, although there have been occasional unconfirmed reports of ostrich sightings in remote areas. Survivors include gazelles, hyenas, and jackals, and there are also small numbers of wild boars, lynxes, and wild cats.

The camel is one well-adapted desert animal. People around the world tend to associate camels with Egypt. These "ships of the desert" were introduced to Egypt as domestic animals around the eighth century B.C.

Egypt has more than 30 species of snakes, half of them venomous. Among the more spectacular species are the horned viper, hooded snake, and Egyptian cobra. There are also many kinds of lizards, scorpions, and insects.

There are some 200 migratory species and 150 resident species of birds. The Nile valley is a major bird migration route between eastern Europe and East Africa. The valley provides food for migrating birds, as they navigate along the river. Some of the most beautiful birds, such as the golden eagle and lammergeier, are found in the Eastern Desert and the Sinai. One of Egypt's most common birds is the hoopoe, a small, colorful ground feeder with a crest-like fan.

The Nile river and the Red Sea coral gardens are home to possibly a thousand marine species, including tiger sharks, moray eels, large perches, carps, and burls.

CAIRO

Cairo, the capital city, is known among Egyptians as the mother of the world. Cairo sits strategically between the valley and delta of the Nile, about a hundred miles from the coast. One out of four Egyptians lives in Cairo, the political and commercial center of the country.

Cairo's population is about 13 million, making it one of the 10 largest cities in the world. The population is increasing at an alarming rate, largely due to people moving in from the countryside to seek work. This has created transportation, housing, and sanitation problems.

The Nile cuts through the city, and there are two large islands, Roda and Gezira. Tahrir, or Liberation, Square is generally considered the city center. Traveling east from Tahrir Square, you pass Opera Square, the Presidential Palace, and beyond that the old city with its wonderful mosques and city gates. The western side has fewer tourist sites but is home to the University of Cairo and the middle-class neighborhoods of Muhandisin and Doqqi. From here, four-lane highways lead to the pyramids on the city's edge. The modern city center is relatively small; apart from one or two wealthy suburbs Cairo is really a great collection of villages in the middle of a vast city.

Cairo by night. Cairo is the capital city of Egypt and is home to nearly 25 percent of the population.

Alexandria was a center of trade and culture in ancient times. It was the capital of Egypt after its founding in 332 B.C. Cleopatra once reigned here as queen.

ALEXANDRIA

Alexandria is Egypt's second largest city with a population of more than 3 million people. It is situated on the northern Mediterranean coast and is a major international harbor. As the name suggests, it was founded by Alexander the Great and in Greek times was an important center of commerce and learning. The Lighthouse of Alexandria once stood here and was considered by some to be one of the Seven Wonders of the Ancient World; the world's first great public library was founded here.

Today Alexandria enjoys a more cosmopolitan atmosphere than the rest of Egypt. The cooling Mediterranean breezes give it a pleasant climate, and many summer homes are built close to the beaches. The city has a good museum and a well-preserved Roman amphitheater.

In addition to the usual forms of transportation, central Alexandria is linked by a tram network. Alexandria is Egypt's chief port and the center of a major industrial region. Businesses in the area take advantage of the city's harbor facilities.

EGYPT'S OTHER CITIES

ASYUT is an important commercial center and university town in central Egypt. It has a large Christian community. Once a major resting point on the caravan route, today Asyut is a center for cotton spinning and pottery.

ASWAN Situated deep in southern Egypt, Aswan is the last major town before the Sudanese border. In ancient times, the pharaohs quarried some of their best granite from this area. Present-day Aswan is famous for the High Dam, and several industries are located here.

A fleet of feluccas on the Nile at Aswan creates a picturesque scene. For thousands of years, feluccas have plied the Nile, using it as a major transportation artery.

LUXOR is a resort town north of Aswan. Luxor's wealth is based on its ancient treasures—it stands on the site of ancient Thebes, the capital of Egypt for much of the pharaonic era. Luxor is linked to Cairo by good rail and road connections, and it has an international airport.

PORT SAID was founded in 1856 as a base for the construction and operation of the Suez Canal. Since then it has grown into a city of nearly half a million people. It is Egypt's second largest port and a free trade zone where many Egyptians go to buy foreign-made electrical goods.

SUEZ and Port Tawfiq guard the southern end of the canal. The ancient Egyptians built a fortress here, and the present city was founded in the 15th century. Although Suez was almost totally destroyed in the 1973 war, the reopening of the canal and the oil boom have seen it prosper. Today it is a thriving city of nearly half a million people.

HISTORY

EGYPT IS THE HOME of one of the world's first great civilizations. An advanced culture that lasted almost 3,000 years developed in the land around 5,000 years ago.

People began to settle along the Nile more than 6,000 years ago. The soil in the river valley was very fertile, and hunter-gatherers gradually abandoned their old way of life to become farmers. The surrounding desert land protected the settlements in the valley from invaders, thus enabling these early inhabitants to prosper. As the population grew, the settlements merged until they formed two kingdoms: one in the valley (Upper Egypt); the other centered in the delta (Lower Egypt).

It is thought that around 2925 B.C. a powerful king known as Menes united the two kingdoms into a single state, creating possibly the first state in human history. A stone palette dating to around that time was discovered at the end of the 19th century A.D. in Kom el Ahmar, an archeological site along the Nile. The Narmer Palette depicts a king wearing the crown of Upper Egypt victorious in battle.

No one is sure who exactly Menes was; he has been linked to two names—Narmer and Aha—inscribed on the Palermo Stone, an ancient record that lists Egypt's kings from the first to fifth dynasties. The king known as Menes founded the first in a line of 30 ancient Egyptian dynasties; he established his capital at Memphis, which is very close to present-day Cairo.

The ancient Egyptians developed many inventions, such as a paper-like material called papyrus, a form of writing that used pictures, a 365-day calendar, and the world's first national government. The Egyptians were also noted mathematicians, poets, doctors, and soldiers. Most of all, the Egyptians are remembered for their building achievements, and their magnificent temples and pyramids remain to tell the tale.

Above: **A detail of a papyrus depiction of an ancient Egyptian.**

Opposite: **A statue of the pharaoh Ramses II at the Temple of Karnak.**

Djoser's Step Pyramid at Saqqara started out as a flat rectangular tomb before taking its final form with six terraces and an almost square base.

OLD KINGDOM (2575–2130 B.C.)

By the end of the third dynasty, around 2575 B.C., Egypt was a firmly established nation with a strong central government. The Old Kingdom rulers also built the greatest monuments that the world had ever seen —the famous pyramids of Egypt.

The first Egyptian pyramid, the Step Pyramid, was a tomb for one of Egypt's greatest kings—Djoser. Redesigned three times, the Step Pyramid eventually rose nearly 200 feet (60 m) in six giant steps. The mastermind behind the Step Pyramid was Imhotep, King Djoser's chief advisor. Apart from being an architect, Imhotep was a priest, scientist, doctor, and writer. So remarkable were his achievements that later generations of Egyptians worshiped him as a god. His masterpiece at Saqqara, the world's oldest all-stone structure of its size, remains a tribute to his genius.

Succeeding pharaohs tried to outdo their predecessors in the size and grandeur of the pyramids that they built. Snefru, the first king of the fourth

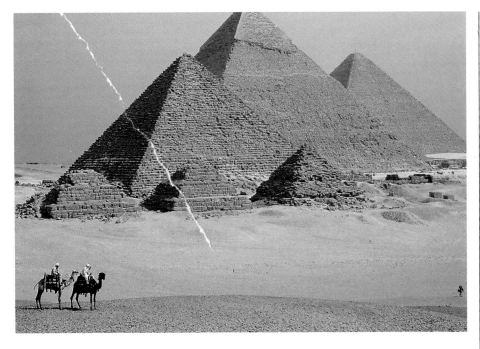

Close to Khufu's Great Pyramid are the smaller pyramids of Khafre and Menkaure at Giza, southwest of Cairo.

dynasty, built several pyramids, including the Bent Pyramid (named so because it angles into a gentler slope about halfway up) and the Red Pyramid (named so because of its pink limestone).

Snefru's monuments were significant achievements, but soon the next king, Khufu, built a bigger pyramid a few miles north. This was the Great Pyramid at Giza. The completed structure reached some 480 feet (146 m) in height. The Great Pyramid is the oldest and only survivor of the Seven Wonders of the Ancient World.

The Old Kingdom was also a time for ambitious exploration: the Egyptians traded actively with Nubia to the south, sent turquoise and copper mining expeditions into the Sinai, and sailed to the Phoenician coast to trade for cedar, olive oil, and wine.

The eighth dynasty saw the last days of the Old Kingdom; Egyptian dynastic history then entered an intermediate period. During the ninth dynasty a power struggle of sorts arose between the pharaohs and some of their high officials, and the pharaohs' pyramids declined while the tombs of local rulers became more elaborate. Widespread conflict gradually led to the formation of twin dynasties.

A painted relief in a pharaonic tomb shows royal subjects bringing gifts, a practice common in ancient Egypt.

MIDDLE KINGDOM (1980–1630 B.C.)

Without an effective central government, Egypt went through a long period of political instability before the competing dynasties were again unified, around 2060 B.C. Mentuhotep, the fourth king of the 11th dynasty, which had its capital at Thebes, and succeeding kings restored Egypt's power and wealth. They rebuilt the central government, sent a large army into Palestine (perhaps to protect trade links), and repaired irrigation systems; Sesostris III built a string of forts to secure Egypt's southern border. During the Middle Kingdom, Egyptian ships sailed as far as Syria, Crete, and Greece.

It was also a golden age for art. Artists produced beautiful royal sculpture, and non-royal people had wooden models of soldiers, houses, and animals placed in their tombs. The Middle Kingdom pharaohs built pyramids almost as large as the great pyramids of the Old Kingdom.

Meanwhile, immigrants were settling in the Nile delta. Toward the end of the Middle Kingdom, around 1630 B.C., the immigrants grew more powerful. From among them a new line of kings arose who threatened the rule of the Egyptian pharaohs in Egypt. This immigrant dynasty was named the Hyksos dynasty, probably derived from an Egyptian term meaning rulers of foreign lands. The Hyksos ruled a large part of Egypt from their capital at Avaris, in the Nile delta, for nearly a century.

NEW KINGDOM (1558–1080 B.C.)

The Hyksos brought new technology to Egypt, particularly in matters of warfare. The horse and chariot was introduced during this period. At the end of the 17th century B.C., the Egyptians ruling from Thebes began

a struggle to drive out the Hyksos. This campaign climaxed during the reign of Ahmose, who reclaimed land that had been under Hyksos rule. Thus began the era of the New Kingdom, when Thebes became the most important city in Egypt.

Often characterized as Egypt's Golden Age, or the Age of Empire, Egypt's New Kingdom lasted about 500 years. Encompassing dynasties 18 through 20, this period of Egyptian history is considered by many scholars to be the high point of ancient Egyptian achievements in art, religion, and literature. Under a series of warrior kings, Egypt became a dominant force in the Near East, with kings from as far away as Syria paying homage to the pharaoh. Egypt also became richer than ever before, with gold, copper, ivory, and ebony pouring in from other lands.

To prevent plunderers from desecrating their treasure-filled tombs, the 18th-dynasty pharaohs invented a new royal burial style. Rather than build an aboveground monument, like a pyramid, they burrowed into the earth and dug out the belowground, hidden tombs that dot the Valley of the Kings.

The temple at Abu Simbel has four 65-foot (20-m) statues of Ramses II, a New Kingdom pharaoh. At the foot of the great statues are smaller ones of the pharaoh's mother and chief wife and a few of his some 100 children.

THE MISSING PHARAOH

Tutankhamen was probably no more than ten years old when he came to the throne. We know very little about the young king, except that he reigned for around eight years and may have died from a head wound caused by a spear or arrow. Compared with many other kings, Tutankhamen had a short and uneventful reign. Yet he was to become the most famous pharaoh of all.

The body of Tutankhamen lay buried in the Valley of the Kings for 3,000 years. Then, in 1922, after years of searching for the missing tomb, an Englishman named Howard Carter made the greatest archeological find of all time.

Together with the pharaoh were thousands of items that had been buried with him, including gold jewelry, statues, thrones, beds, and a golden mask. There were also bunches of dried flowers, picked fresh the day the king had been buried. We can only wonder who placed this touching gift among all the gold and finery.

AMENHOTEP IV In the middle of the 14th century B.C. Amenhotep IV threw Egypt into turmoil by raising the status of the sun god, Aton, to that of supreme god of the universe. Amenhotep IV changed his name to Akhenaton, which meant servant of the Aton, and assumed the power of the priestly class. He also built a new capital city at Amarna.

This was a wonderful time for artists, who were allowed to explore different styles. The resulting art of Amarna thus had a more natural, less contrived appearance. However, rivalry between Akhenaton and the priests of the old, polytheistic religion created civil unrest, and domestic problems weakened Egypt's power in the near east and led to the loss of land in Syria. Akhenaton's religion died with him; his successor, the child king Tutankhamen, was forced by the priests to revive the old religion.

RAMSES II In accomplishments, Ramses II may be ranked as one of the most important and effective rulers of the ancient world. Truly deserving of his nickname, "the Great," Ramses II had the longest recorded reign (67 years), fought more battles, and produced more statuary and buildings than any other ruler of ancient Egypt. He also fathered more than 100 children and lived to be over 90 years of age.

Shortly after coming to the throne, Ramses II initiated what was to be the most-recorded military campaign in the history of the ancient Near East—the Battle of Kadesh, fought against the Hittites. Both sides claimed victory, and conflicts continued afterward. Eventually the warring nations agreed to the terms of peace. A record of the peace treaty appears on the walls of a few Egyptian temples and on Hittite clay tablets. The rest of Ramses' reign was marked more by domestic building projects and diplomatic successes than by military activities.

EGYPT FALLS TO FOREIGN RULE

The New Kingdom ended around 1075 B.C. Egypt was split in two parts, one ruled by pharaohs, the other by priests. The country gradually fell to invaders, such as the Assyrians and Persians, who founded their own short-lived lines of kings in Egypt. In 332 B.C. Alexander the Great swept in from Macedonia with his army and absorbed Egypt into his vast empire. He stayed in Egypt for a while and founded the city of Alexandria. After his death in 323 B.C., his general Ptolemy began a new line of rulers in Egypt.

The last of the Ptolemies, Cleopatra VII, ruled in the first century B.C. Cleopatra VII formed an alliance with Julius Caesar and then with Mark Antony, co-ruler of Rome with Octavian. Cleopatra and Mark Antony sailed to battle against Octavian at Actium, Greece, but were defeated. They fled to Alexandria, where they committed suicide the following year.

Egypt then came under Roman rule. Like the Greeks before them, the Romans left the Egyptians to their ancient religion. That changed with the arrival of Christianity, and from the fourth century A.D. Egypt was rapidly converted to a Christian country.

The Ptolemaic rulers governed Egypt for three centuries, from the new city of Alexandria. They built the Library of Alexandria, which housed the greatest works of science and the arts. Egypt's capital also became an economic hub, producing practical and luxury goods such as papyrus and perfume, and serving as a port for goods moving between Africa and Europe.

ISLAMIC EGYPT

When the Roman empire split in A.D. 395, Egypt went to the Byzantine (eastern Roman) emperors. Byzantine rule continued until around A.D. 639, when Egypt fell to the Arabs. The Arabs established their capital at Fustat, which would grow into the great city of Cairo. They influenced the people of Egypt more than any of the earlier conquerors did—most Egyptians embraced Islam, and Arabic became widely spoken.

Under the Arabs, Egypt became part of the Islamic empire. First the Umayyad dynasty ruled the province from Damascus; then Egypt came under the jurisdiction of the Baghdad-based Abbasid dynasty.

From A.D. 868 to 969, the Turkish dynasties of Tulunid and Ikhshidid had autonomous rule over Egypt, while still acknowledging Baghdad's authority. But in A.D. 973 the Shi'a Muslim Fatimids established their own caliphate, independent of the Sunni Muslim Abbasids. The Fatimids had their capital in Cairo (Al Kahira in Arabic, meaning the conqueror), which has been the capital ever since.

In the 12th century, Crusaders from Europe invaded Egypt, and the caliph of Syria sent the Fatimids military assistance. A Kurdish general, Salah ad Din ibn Ayyub (better known as Saladin), defeated the Crusaders. However, in 1171 Saladin overthrew the Fatimids and founded the Ayyubid dynasty. He returned Egypt to Sunni Islam and in 1187 drove the Crusaders out of Jerusalem, thus becoming a hero of the Islamic world. His descendants employed Turkish slaves—Mamluks—as bodyguards. Being very loyal, the Mamluks quickly rose to high positions in the army and government, and in 1250, loyalty aside, the Mamluks seized the sultanate.

The Ibn Tulun Mosque, completed in A.D. 879, is one of Cairo's oldest. It was built by Ahmad Ibn Tulun, who was sent by the Abbasid caliph in A.D. 868 to govern Egypt. Ibn Tulun later founded the Tulunid dynasty.

WESTERN CONTACT

The Mamluks ruled until 1517, when they were overthrown by the Ottoman Turks. Egypt faded from the focus of world events under Ottoman rule in the 16th and 17th centuries. Then in 1798 the country made a dramatic comeback to the world stage, when it was invaded by French forces led by Napoleon Bonaparte.

Bonaparte hoped to create a French colony and disrupt England's communications with the British empire in India. His hopes were dashed when a British fleet led by Lord Nelson defeated the French fleet a month later. The next year Bonaparte returned to France, and in 1801 British and Ottoman forces drove the French out of Egypt.

In 1803 the British left Egypt, leaving the land to the Ottoman Turks, whose army maintained control over Egypt. However, a young Albanian officer in the army—Muhammad Ali—challenged the Ottoman Turks. In 1805, after a revolt against the Ottoman ruler, Ali was declared Egypt's new leader. He developed a centralized government system and increased contact with the West.

In the hands of Ali's successors, Egypt became increasingly more Westernized. Ali's fourth son, Said, ruled from 1854 to 1863. He permitted France to construct a canal across the Suez. This would make Egypt strategically important to the great European powers, but it would also make the country increasingly vulnerable to political events elsewhere.

Lavish spending put Egypt into debt, and in 1875 its rulers sold their shares in the Suez Canal to Britain. British influence in Egypt grew so strong that they were soon interfering in Egypt's domestic issues. Anti-British uprisings led to a British military invasion. Although the British made good reforms in areas such as banking, they neglected education and public health, and an independence movement began to develop.

Muhammad Ali (1769–1849) was a dynamic leader who initiated Egypt's first modernization program. He created new ministries and schools, built canals, introduced cotton to the country, and developed a textile industry. By the time of his death, Egypt had acquired an international standing.

THE STRUGGLE FOR INDEPENDENCE

As World War I broke out in 1914, Britain declared Egypt a protectorate and sent troops to guard the Suez Canal. This intensified anti-British sentiments in Egypt and strengthened the nationalist movement led by Saad Zaghlul. Britain granted Egypt independence in 1922, but kept the right to station troops in the country. During World War II, hundreds of thousands of British troops passed through the country.

Egypt emerged from World War II determined to rid itself of foreign influence. It devoted itself to the Arab cause and was involved in the formation of the Arab League. In 1948, when Palestine was divided into Arab and Jewish states, Egypt joined Iraq, Jordan, and Syria in the war against Israel. Egypt's defeat triggered riots in the country, until in 1952 a group of army officers headed by Colonel Gamal Abdel Nasser seized power and started to tackle Egypt's serious social problems. A major reform was the Land Act, which broke up the big estates and gave land to the fellahin, Egypt's farm laborers.

On the international scene, Nasser negotiated a withdrawal of British troops by 1956.

LEADING THE ARAB CAUSE

Egypt's relationship with Israel remained hostile long after World War II. As a leader of the Arab world, Egypt wished to see the land of Israel returned to the Palestinians. In 1967 President Nasser entered a military alliance with Syria and Jordan and closed the Gulf of Aqaba to Israeli shipping. The Israelis, seeing the blockade as an act of war, launched an attack on Egypt, destroying most of the Egyptian air force on the ground. Israel defeated Egypt in the Six-Day War, taking the Sinai and closing the Suez Canal.

After this crushing defeat, President Nasser offered to resign, but mass public support persuaded him to stay. The Soviet Union gave military equipment worth millions of dollars to rebuild the Egyptian army. After several border incidents threatened to restart the war, the United States and the United Nations arranged a ceasefire.

In 1970, after Nasser's death, Anwar al-Sadat became president. He ordered an attack on Israel in 1973, and Egyptian troops stormed the fortifications along the Suez Canal and overran the Sinai. Although the Israeli army, supplied with a massive airlift by the United States, struck back and regained much lost ground, Egyptians had gained a renewed confidence in their military capability and felt strong enough to seek peace. In 1977 President Sadat made a historic visit to Jerusalem. In 1978 Egypt and Israel signed the Camp David accords, in which Israel returned the rest of the Sinai (having returned part of it in 1975). Then in 1979 the two countries concluded a peace treaty, the first between Israel and an Arab nation. This greatly angered the Arab world, and Egypt was dismissed from the Arab League. Many Egyptians were also furious, and in 1981 President Sadat was assassinated by extremists at a military parade.

Hosni Mubarak, Sadat's successor, continued to maintain diplomatic ties with Israel and to move closer to the United States and the Western world. Relations with many Arab nations also gradually improved, and Egypt's role in the Israeli-Palestinian conflict grew in importance. In 1989 Egypt rejoined the Arab League.

Egypt has played a crucial role in conflicts in the Middle East. During the gulf war in 1991, President Mubarak tried to mediate a settlement between Iraq and Kuwait, failing which Egypt sent troops to support a massive coalition to free Kuwait from Iraqi occupation; and in 1993 Egypt facilitated a peace accord between Israel and the Palestine Liberation Organization.

A leading member of the revolution that overthrew the monarchy in 1952, Nasser introduced many reforms when he became president. Among his accomplishments was the Aswan High Dam.

29

GOVERNMENT

EGYPT WAS A CONSTITUTIONAL MONARCHY headed by a king until 1952, when a group of army officers seized control of the government. King Farouk went into exile, and the following year Egypt became a republic headed by a president.

President Nasser adopted socialist policies, which emphasized state planning, public sector involvement in the development of industry, and populist reforms. In the 1970s President Sadat introduced a more open policy, encouraging foreign investment and private initiative. President Mubarak maintained the major lines of Sadat's policy.

THE EGYPTIAN PRESIDENT

The president of the Arab Republic of Egypt must be Egyptian and born of Egyptian parents. He or she must also be at least 40 years old. The presidential candidate must be nominated by at least two-thirds of the legislature and elected by more than 50 percent of the legislature. The legislature-elected candidate must be approved in a public referendum. The president is elected for a six-year term and can serve an additional term after that.

The Egyptian president exercises broad powers. He appoints and dismisses the prime minister and other ministers, and he can appoint one or more vice-presidents; with the cabinet, he defines the general state policy and oversees its implementation. The president is the supreme commander of the armed forces; when necessary, and with the approval of the legislature, he can declare war.

Over the years, the Arab Republic of Egypt has also granted more political freedom to its people. When deciding on important matters relating to the country's interest, the Egyptian president calls for a referendum of the people.

Above: **The first Arab leader to visit Israel, Anwar al-Sadat received the 1978 Nobel Peace Prize jointly with Israel's prime minister, Menachem Begin.**

Opposite: **The Republican Palace in Cairo.**

Mubarak, one of Sadat's most trusted colleagues, took over the presidency after Sadat's death.

EXECUTIVE BRANCH

The cabinet, called the Council of Ministers, consists of the prime minister—the head of government—and his ministers and deputies.

The Council oversees the various ministries, issues decrees, drafts laws, and draws up the general budget and state plan.

LEGISLATURE

Egypt's bicameral legislature consists of the People's Assembly and the Advisory Council.

The People's Assembly has 454 members; 444 are elected by popular vote and 10 are appointed by the president. The appointed members usually represent the Coptic minority, women, and the youth, while at least half of the elected members must be workers or farmers. Members of the assembly serve five-year terms.

The People's Assembly supervises the executive authority, approves the general state plan and budget, and proposes laws. The assembly has the power to approve or reject draft laws through a majority vote by its members who are present during the sessions.

The Advisory Council has 264 members, of whom 176 are elected by popular vote and 88 are appointed by the president. The council is a respected advisory body, but it has no legislative authority. It considers matters such as the constitution, new laws, or any policy referred to it by the president.

Members of the council serve six-year terms; half of the membership changes every three years. The last mid-term election of the council was in 2001. The council now has 15 women members.

JUDICIARY

The court system in Egypt consists of administrative courts and courts of general jurisdiction. In addition, there are special courts such as labor tribunals and family or security courts. The Supreme Constitutional Court is the highest court in the republic. It reviews the constitutionality of the rulings of the lower courts and settles disputes between them.

Prior to the 1952 revolution, there was a separate system of religious courts that enforced family law (marriage, divorce, and inheritance) and handled religious endowments or trusts. *Shariah* (SHAH-ri-ah) courts had jurisdiction over Muslims, while Copts had their own courts. In 1953 religious courts were abolished and their functions transferred to the secular court system. However, the secular courts continued to refer to Islamic law, especially in family law. Egypt amended its constitution in 1980, making Islamic law the basis of national law.

GOVERNORATES

At the regional level, Egypt is divided into 26 administrative units called governorates: Ad Daqahliyah, Al Bahr al Ahmar, Al Buhayrah, Al Fayyum, Al Gharbiyah, Al Iskandariyah, Al Isma'iliyah, Al Jizah, Al Minufiyah, Al Minya, Al Qahirah, Al Qalyubiyah, Al Wadi al Jadid, Ash Sharqiyah, As Suways, Aswan, Asyut, Bani Suwayf, Bur Sa'id, Dumyat, Janub Sina', Kafr ash Shaykh, Matruh, Qina, Shamal Sina', and Suhaj.

Each governorate has a governor appointed by the president. The governor works with an elected council to manage matters such as the building of a new hospital or school. Each governorate consists of smaller administrative units, such as districts and villages. These are managed by mayors with their own elected councils.

A monument at the High Dam at Aswan commemorates the friendship between Egypt and the Soviet Union. The dam was built with Soviet aid, after the Western powers refused to assist.

FOREIGN POLICY

According to the Egyptian geographer-historian Gamal Hemdan, the geopolitical history of Egypt has made it moderate, tolerant, and a compromise seeker. Being at the heart of a region where many cultural and political movements have taken place has made Egypt a leader both in the region and in the world.

Egypt continues to play such a leading role today; following the 1952 revolution, it defined three foreign-policy circles that reflect its Middle Eastern, African, and international identities.

THE ARAB-MIDDLE EASTERN CIRCLE dominates Egyptian foreign policy. Since the establishment of the Arab League in 1945, Egypt has placed Arab issues among its main interests. Egypt's role in the 1948 Arab-Israeli war demonstrated Egypt's sense of belonging in the Arab world.

However, Egypt's commitment to the Israeli peace process since the 1970s strained its relations with the Arab states. Hence, Egypt sought to strike a fragile balance in its Middle Eastern policy decisions, working to restore Arab relations on the one hand and pushing forward with the Israeli peace process on the other.

Egypt's Middle Eastern policy has achieved tremendous success, renewing and strengthening Arab cohesion while leading the way to peaceful relations with Israel. Egypt has also supported the struggle for independence in other Arab countries.

THE AFRICAN CIRCLE Egypt was in many ways an African superpower in the 1960s, supporting liberation movements all over the continent. In 1963 Egypt became a founding member of the Organization of African Unity.

Since then Egypt has been keeping track of events in many African nations, from Angola to Zaire (since 1997 the Democratic Republic of Congo), calling on factions to turn to law rather than violence in settling political disputes.

At the same time, Egypt maintains a policy of non-intervention with regard to the domestic affairs of its African neighbors.

THE INTERNATIONAL CIRCLE Egypt maintains almost 170 embassies around the world in its desire to promote cordial relations with nations all over the globe.

Egypt also participates in many international organizations. It was a founding member of the United Nations in 1945 and of the Non-Aligned Movement in 1955. In 1994 Alexandria hosted the first meeting of the Mediterranean Forum, also known as Foromed, which aims to promote understanding and cooperation among nations in the Mediterranean. Algeria, France, Greece, Italy, Malta, Morocco, Portugal, Spain, Tunisia, and Turkey are Foromed's other members.

Egypt takes a strong stand against terrorism. President Mubarak has called for nuclear disarmament in the Middle East and international cooperation in fighting terrorism, meeting with world leaders to discuss ways to combat the global threat.

In 1973 Egyptian forces stormed Israeli fortifications on the Suez Canal in a surprise assault on the Sinai. Their success enabled President Sadat to initiate peace talks with Israel.

ECONOMY

WITH THE SECOND largest economy in the Arab world, Egypt has four main foreign exchange earners: oil exports, Suez Canal tolls, tourism receipts, and money sent to Egypt by Egyptians working abroad. Services make up the biggest economic sector, accounting for about half the gross domestic product (GDP). Next in importance is industry, about a third of the GDP. Agriculture's share of the GDP is about one-fifth.

FINDING LAND FOR AGRICULTURE

Although other sectors have overtaken it as a money earner, agriculture remains one of the mainstays of the Egyptian economy. It is the largest employer, providing jobs to about a third of the population. Apart from direct employment in agriculture, agro-based industries and services are also very important to Egypt's economic prospects.

Egypt has approximately 12,969 square miles (33,589 square km) of land under cultivation. Given the shortage of arable land, the Egyptian government has paid special attention to reclaiming desert land, as it did through the building of the Aswan High Dam in the 1950s. Reclamation projects have helped to create new agricultural land, but settlement expansion also competes for more land. In addition, poor drainage has raised salinity levels in some areas, hindering attempts to cultivate crops as far as was thought possible with land reclamation projects.

Because Egypt has virtually no rain, all crops depend on irrigation. Egypt has been drawing water from the Nile since pharaonic times. And since the construction of the Aswan High Dam, Lake Nasser has been storing excess floodwater, forming the world's largest manmade lake in the process. This floodwater provides for the country's water needs all year. Lake Nasser has also inspired the government to launch one of the most ambitious agricultural projects in the world—Toshka.

Above: **Orange pickers. Agriculture in Egypt is done more on a commercial than a subsistence basis. Exports of crops such as oranges, onions, potatoes, and tomatoes have expanded rapidly.**

Opposite: **A street market in Cairo.**

Loading sugarcane for transportation. Other crops such as wheat, barley, potatoes, beans, rice, and onions are also cultivated for export and for home consumption.

TOSHKA is one of the greatest attempts by the Egyptians to expand beyond the Nile valley, the center of Egyptian civilization for centuries. The Toshka project has been called President Mubarak's great pyramid.

The project is based on the idea of opening a long canal from a huge overflow basin to divert water from Lake Nasser to irrigate more than 840 square miles (2,175 square km). Construction began in 1997 and is expected to be completed by 2017. The aim is to extend the area suitable for settlement to about 25 percent of Egypt's land, providing homes for millions in the 21st century and beyond. The area will produce food for both domestic consumption and export.

The Toshka project will change the population map of Egypt—it will create a large populated area in the Western Desert northwest of Abu Simbel, near the Sudanese border.

IRRIGATING THE LAND

More and more water is being pumped from the Nile with the help of modern machines. However, the Egyptians still use some ancient irrigation methods. One example is the *shadoof* (shah-DOOF), which consists of a bucket at the end of a long pole that is dipped into the water and counterbalanced with a large stone (*right*).

Another ancient tool used to irrigate land is the *sakiya* (sah-KEE-yah). This is a vertical waterwheel with buckets or pots attached to it. The waterwheel is driven by a donkey or water buffalo, and as it turns the vessels collect water on the way up and drop it into a small canal on the way down.

The Archimedean screw is an ingenious invention. When turned, the screw action forces water through the tube. An Archimedean screw can irrigate 32,670 square feet (3,035 square m) of land a day.

CROPS AND LANDOWNERS

Cotton, rice, corn, and sorghum are Egypt's main summer crops, while wheat, vegetables, and Egyptian clover are the main winter crops. Egypt is self-sufficient in fruit and vegetables, but overall food production has lagged behind the needs of a rapidly growing population. Today, Egypt imports about 60 percent of its food.

Cotton is the main cash crop, accounting for nearly a fifth of Egypt's export earnings and providing the base for the domestic spinning and weaving industry.

The 1952 land reforms divided the big farms of rich landowners into small units and gave them to the fellahin. Farmers sell cotton, sugarcane, and half their rice harvest to the government. However, as the fellahin's land is too small to introduce modern farming methods, they still rely heavily on manual labor.

Iron ore, mined in the Western desert, provides the raw material for the country's iron and steel industries.

MANUFACTURING

During the mid-1990s, the government launched a privatization program to transfer the ownership and operation of factories from the public sector to the private. Most factories at the time were still owned or supervised by the government. Since the revolution, the public sector had to lead the country in the push for industrialization.

Privatization measures have managed to raise the productivity of factories, which are beginning to see profits after years of losses. However, the government still holds major factories and companies, such as car assembly lines and iron and steel production plants, for which there are reform plans to improve their performance.

Manufacturing accounts for 20 percent of Egypt's production. In the past decade, many new industries have been introduced in the country and existing ones improved. Ceramics, plastics, petrochemicals, iron, steel, aluminum, cement, paper, fertilizer, textiles and fabrics, clothes, leather goods, cars, electronics, furniture, and processed foods are just some products bearing the "Made in Egypt" label. Computer software is the newest addition to Egyptian manufacturing. While agriculture is no longer the backbone of the Egyptian economy, manufacturing industries that depend mainly on agricultural produce are still important.

The government is also trying to develop industry in the new cities outside the traditional population centers of Cairo and Alexandria. The government has built hundreds of new factories in these new cities and is offering investment incentives and improving infrastructure to attract investors and workers.

Fabrics are sold in many shops and markets in Egypt. First developed by Muhammad Ali, Egypt's textile production has become a major manufacturing industry.

INTERNATIONAL TRADE

From the 1950s to the end of the 1980s, most of Egypt's manufacturing exports went to the Soviet Union and eastern Europe. Today, the United States and western Europe form the main export market for Egyptian manufactured goods.

With a growing export market, Egypt has had to work hard to bring its products up to international standards. Partnership agreements with the European Union and the United States and new investment laws are boosting the quantity and quality of Egyptian manufacturing.

Despite the growing number of factories and the rising standard of Egyptian products, Egypt still has to import many items, such as food, machinery, chemicals, wood, paper, and metal products. In fact, Egypt buys more than it can sell each year. Egypt imports mainly from the European Union and the United States, as well as from other Middle Eastern countries and some Asian nations.

A rig drills a well off the coast of the Sinai. Most of Egypt's oil reserves are located offshore.

OIL AND GAS

The history of oil in Egypt dates back to 1868, when the Sulfur Mines Company discovered oil near Dumiat, on the Mediterranean coast. However, the first oil field in that area was only found in 1908. Egypt pioneered oil refining in the Middle East in 1913.

Today, oil generates about 40 percent of Egypt's export revenue. The oil industry is largely controlled by the Egyptian General Petroleum Corporation, a state-owned organization. It works with the private sector in the exploration, processing, and distribution of oil and oil products.

Egypt's oil is found mainly in the Gulf of Suez, the Western and Eastern deserts, and the Sinai desert. The Gulf of Suez produces almost 70 percent of the nation's oil. The gulf's oil comes from both offshore fields, such as Ramadan and October, and onshore fields (on the eastern bank), such as Ras Gharib and Karim.

Today, Egypt produces around 34 million tons (34 billion kg) of oil a year, 65 percent of which is used domestically, with the surplus exported mainly to Europe and North America.

Gas was first discovered in Egypt in 1967. Further finds were made in the 1980s in the Nile delta and the Western Desert, but the gas industry still has great potential for growth. About 60 percent of the country's gas is used to generate power; the rest goes mainly to industrial use.

A network of pipelines transports crude oil and natural gas from the fields to the refineries to domestic consumers or to pipelines connecting Egypt to its export markets.

TOURISM

Egypt was one of the earliest nations to develop a booming tourist trade—during the days of steamship travel, passengers sailing through the Suez Canal often made a detour to visit the pyramids.

Today, tourism is Egypt's second most important foreign revenue earner, after oil. The modern tourist industry is served by a range of hotels of different standards and by airlines. Egypt Air and internal carriers transport passengers quickly between Cairo and other world capitals and between major cities in Egypt.

A tour guide explains the significance of a temple painting to a group of tourists.

Within a city, fleets of comfortable buses transport visitors from one site to the next.

Tourism is the ideal industry for Egypt; it employs many people and earns vital foreign exchange. Egypt's top tourist destinations are Cairo, where most visitors look for the pyramids and the National Museum's Tutankhamen collection, and Luxor, where ancient temple ruins are the main attraction. The Sinai is also a popular area, where people enjoy snorkeling and diving or climbing Mount Sinai.

Unfortunately, Egypt's tourist industry suffers from instability in the region. Terrorist activity in the Middle East and the wars in Iraq caused the Egyptian economy a serious loss of tourism revenue and made life harder for the many people who had come to depend on the trade. Egyptian tourism was doing better after 2000, receiving almost 5 million tourists the first two years. Today, tourist facilities that provide information about historical and monumental sites, and many entertainment and leisure facilities give tourists a relaxing and enjoyable vacation. But the war in Iraq and increased terrorism have made the future uncertain.

ENVIRONMENT

THE CONCEPT OF environmental protection may have been born in ancient Egypt. The religious beliefs of ancient Egyptians showed a respect for nature. An Egyptian religious text indicates that a person seeking forgiveness from the gods had to declare in front of a priest not only that he or she had never killed or stolen, but also that he or she had never altered the water of the Nile River.

Even today, it is widely believed in Egyptian cultural tradition that the earth and everything on it, such as water and air, are God's gifts to the human race that we are to preserve in gratitude.

However, the current condition of the natural environment in Egypt does not reflect this belief. Conservation in a densely populated country with sandy desert covering most of the land is extremely challenging. Compared to land that is newly settled, land that has been inhabited for a long time tends to be more susceptible to damage by human activity. Many parts of Egypt, especially along the Nile, have been continuously inhabited by people for more than 7,000 years. It is thus reasonable to expect environmental problems in the major cities, which have a long history of human settlement.

Nonetheless, the government and nongovernmental organizations (NGOs) are making some effort to address the country's environmental problems, with valid urgency. Prolonged environmental damage has resulted in the destruction of wildlife, poor health, and the accelerated deterioration of ancient monuments, the nation's pride and heritage. These problems have become a fact of life in Egypt's crowded cities and are likely to get worse unless measures are taken to raise awareness, change settlement patterns, reduce pollution, and improve systems of garbage disposal, among other things. Financial aid from nations such as the United States is also helping Egypt achieve its environmental goals.

Opposite: **A diver enjoys the beauty of nature in the waters off the Sinai coast.**

Tour boats on the Red Sea. Careful planning and control of tourist activity is becoming crucial as coastal resorts such as Hurghada and Sharm el Sheikh draw more and more tourists.

POLLUTION

In a large city such as Cairo there are many sources of pollution: domestic waste generated by almost 18 million people living and working in the capital; exhaust fumes from the more than 2 million cars traveling the streets daily; and effluents released by factories into the air and waterways. It has been estimated that more than 230 billion gallons (around 870 billion liters) of industrial pollutants enter the waters of the Nile every year, the equivalent of more than 630 million gallons (around 2.4 billion liters) on average per day.

As the established cities get more and more crowded, green spaces shrink, exacerbating the air pollution problem. In Cairo, especially, this has reduced the purifying effect of the trees on the air that the inhabitants breathe every day. Air pollutants expose people to the risk of illness. More lethal than sand blown from the open desert are metal compounds suspended in the air. The air in Cairo has among the highest levels of lead particles in the world.

The treatment and disposal of solid waste in Egypt is formally carried out by the public sector. But private companies are sometimes hired to collect refuse in certain areas, such as hotels and airports, while foreign companies manage municipal solid waste in Cairo, Alexandria, and Giza. Most of Egypt's garbage is incinerated at open dumpsites, which adds to air pollution. To alleviate the problem of disposal, plants are being built to recycle refuse or convert organic waste to fertilizer.

ERODING HISTORY Another serious consequence of air pollution in Egypt is its effect on the country's ancient monuments. Perhaps the most famous proof of the effects of pollution on Egypt's pharaonic treasures is the Sphinx at Giza, whose face has been scoured and scarred by sand and other particles in the air. In the 1980s, in a bid to rescue one of the most precious symbols of the nation's history, the government initiated a 10-year restoration project involving local and international architects and archeologists. Repair work continues as the monument grows older and less resistant to archeological pollution.

Ruins of the temple of Tuthmosis III at Karnak. Egypt's archeological treasures suffer daily the effects of erosive particles in the air.

ENVIRONMENTAL POLICY

Until recently, the environment was not high on the list of the Egyptian government's pressing issues. In the past decade Egyptian policy makers have paid much more attention to environmental issues. Even so, not many Egyptians are truly aware of the urgency of environmental protection in their country.

The government has thus taken the lead in trying to slow down the destruction of nature's gifts to the nation. In 1982 an institute for environmental studies was set up, followed in 1994 by the Egyptian Environmental Affairs Agency (EEAA). In 1997 the EEAA became an executive arm of the Ministry of State for Environmental Affairs (MSEA).

In addition to conducting environmental research, the MSEA develops environmental awareness and education campaigns, works with other environmental bodies, monitors industrial waste management, manages nature reserves, and generally sets standards for environmental protection in Egypt.

This has not been an easy job for the government in the light of Egypt's economic circumstances. It took years for the public to give the Environment Act of 1994 the same amount of respect as other laws. To convince the people to join in national environmental protection efforts, the government has had to explain how its environmental policies had economic benefits as well. For example, policies promoting efficient use of natural resources can help both the environment and the economy by reducing monetary expenditure as well as carbon dioxide emissions.

State budget allocations and donations from Egyptian and foreign environmental bodies finance the Environmental Protection Fund. International support is an important component of the government's mission to save Egypt's natural environment. The United States, for example, works with the Egyptian government to run the Egyptian Environmental Policy Program (EEPP).

Opposite: **Traffic in Alexandria. Egyptian drivers have switched to unleaded gas, and airborne lead levels have fallen dramatically since the Environment Act of 1994.**

Below: **A boat party off the Sinai coast. With the fast growth of tourism in the southern Sinai, tour operators are trained to ensure that environmental rules are followed.**

WILDLIFE PROTECTION

A drive in the deserts of Egypt runs through awesome landscapes with curious wildlife; a dive in the Red Sea reveals picture-perfect scenes of colorful coral reefs, with equally colorful creatures such as clown fish swimming among anemone (*below*).

Egypt's wildlife is as precious a treasure as the nation's ancient monuments. Unfortunately, Egypt's plants and animals have fallen victim to pollution as have the pharaonic ruins. The UNEP World Conservation Monitoring Center has classified as threatenened 15 species of mammals, 11 bird species, 6 species of reptiles, and around 80 plant species in Egypt.

Another threat to Egyptian wildlife is the international black market in endangered species. Egypt has long been a transit point for the illegal wildlife trade in Africa and Asia. Trade in endangered flora and fauna is officially banned in Egypt, but enforcement of the law is difficult, given a lack of financial resources and public awareness.

A member of the Convention on International Trade in Endangered Species of Wild Flora and Fauna (CITES) since 1978, Egypt has recently stepped up its efforts to comply more actively with the convention, which requires member nations to protect their own endangered species both within and beyond their borders.

ENVIRONMENTAL PROJECTS

The Egyptian government's most significant environmental projects to date include the establishment of 76 monitoring stations to measure air pollution, public environmental education and training campaigns, and the establishment of 21 nature reserves.

Egypt's protected areas occupy 8.5 percent of the nation's total land area and represent a variety of ecosystems. More sites will eventually receive protected status.

Two famous nature reserves in Egypt are the Ras Muhammad National Park at the tip of the Sinai and the Saint Catherine Protectorate in the central-southern Sinai. The 185-square mile (around 480-square km) Ras Muhammad National Park includes the Tiran and Sanafir islands. It is a haven for rare corals and numerous fish and birds. The 2,220-square mile (5,750-square km) Saint Catherine Protectorate is home to high-altitude mammals such as foxes, hyenas, wildcats, and wolves, reptiles such as snakes and geckos, and many kinds of insects.

Lake Qarun in Al Fayyum is an important wetland area populated by a wide variety of fish and birds such as ducks, eagles, flamingoes, and swans. Lake Qarun is also special for its fossils, some dating back to over 30 million years ago.

Tree-planting projects are another way in which the government and NGOs are trying to improve the environment in Egypt. The First Lady, Suzanne Mubarak, sponsored the planting of one million trees in the city of Heliopolis near Cairo, through the Society for the Development of Services. On a larger scale, the government has started a project, using a special watering gel developed by a U.S. company, to plant 17 million olive, orange, and other trees in and around the new city 6th of October, outside Cairo.

In 2002 Egypt hosted the first international conference on Protected Areas and Sustainable Development. Participants came from all over the world to attend the forum, held at Sharm El-Sheikh, where over 200 studies were recorded, adding to the world's knowledge of protected areas, ecotourism, and biodiversity.

EGYPTIANS

AROUND 90 PERCENT of Egypt's population are Hamitic Arabs—people from a line of intermarriages between the ancient Egyptian Hamites and Arabs who came to Egypt from the seventh century onward. The ancient Egyptians belonged to the eastern branch of a people known as Hamites (the northern Hamites formed the other branch). Hamitic peoples are descendents of Ham, one of Noah's three sons.

However, although Egypt is categorized as an Arab nation, Egyptians take pride in their history and culture and consider themselves unique.

There have been many other ethnic influences, due to a long history of immigration and interaction with other Middle Eastern, Arab, and European peoples. Apart from the Hamitic Arabs, there are also Nubian and European minorities in the Egyptian population. Some dark-skinned Egyptians have traces of Nubian blood, while some lighter-skinned Egyptians are of Turkish descent. There are even some Egyptians who have blond hair, owing to their Syrian or European genes.

Egypt's ethnic minorities generally do not face major sociopolitical problems. Small groups such as the Nubians and the Bedouins are also increasingly assimilating into mainstream Egyptian society. The Nubians, from the deep south of Egypt, have been interacting more widely with other Egyptians since the construction of the High Dam, and many Bedouins, originally desert nomads, have settled in villages in the oases and in the Sinai.

Fellahin make up a large majority of the population. They are the farmers of the Nile valley and delta; the name fellahin comes from the Arabic word *felaha* (feh-LAH-ha), meaning to labor or till the earth.

Above: **Coptic Christians buy communion bread outside a church. Copts, mostly in Asyut, Luxor, Cairo, and Alexandria, make up 15 percent of Egypt's population.**

Opposite: **An Egyptian sits among ancient ruins.**

53

A fellahin leads his faithful cargo carrier.

FELLAHIN

Of all modern-day Egyptians, the fellahin are perhaps the closest descendants of the ancient Egyptians. The fellahin have been described as the "true" Egyptians. Over the centuries, they have only occasionally inter-married with African, Turkish, and Arab people.

Most fellahin live in small villages. Their houses are often single-story buildings with thick walls made of unbaked mud bricks (although newer homes may use cement). The family may keep goats, chickens, sheep, or water buffaloes in the yard at night. The fellahin depend on the land for their livelihood.

The fellahin lifestyle might appear to have changed little for centuries—pictures on ancient tomb walls of people farming seem to come alive in the Egyptian countryside. But in fact, living standards have improved in the last 40 years. Almost every village has at least a central well or fountain providing clean water, and villagers have an electrical supply and access to radio or television.

Most villages have basic healthcare available. Before the revolution, the only schools were those run by the mosques. Today, virtually every village child has the opportunity to attend a government school.

Until the 1970s Egyptians in the villages used to marry within their communities. However, with increasing rural-to-urban migration and improvements in transportation, the Egyptian peasants began looking for their life partners in other villages and even in the cities. Apart from their religion, which does not allow interreligious marriage, younger fellahin are relatively open in choosing their life partners.

THE EGYPTIAN CHARACTER

The Egyptian character has largely been influenced by the village environment. A readiness to help one another, originating from the harshness of rural life, has become a national characteristic. Even in Cairo, a modern city, someone in trouble—perhaps hurt in an accident—is likely to be helped by passers-by.

Another Egyptian trait is resilience, stemming perhaps from centuries of suffering and poverty. Egyptians have an ability to stay positive and to persevere through bad times. But they can also be extremely excitable, ready to argue and shout over small everyday matters. Fortunately, they are usually just as quick to embrace and forgive.

Egyptians have a great sense of humor. Jests and practical jokes are appreciated with loud infectious laughter. Political jokes are popular and often very clever, yet politics is not the only source of joke material. Unfortunately, some jokes poke fun at a certain section of the population. In particular, city folk have a large collection of jokes about fellahin, Egypt's rural peasants. However, many Egyptians in the cities also admire and respect fellahin for their common sense and determination.

Egyptians identify themselves usually as Egyptian and seldom as Arab.

Perhaps the single most uniting factor among the Egyptian people is their pride in their country, in their land, in the "Egyptian way." Possibly all Egyptians, even if they live in the cities, consider themselves "people of the land."

A Sinai Bedouin, covered to protect herself from the strong rays of the sun as she gathers firewood. Romanticized portrayals of Bedouin nomads gloss over the harsh reality of desert life.

BEDOUINS

The Bedouins are the most distinct tribal community in Egypt. They lived traditionally in the Western and Sinai deserts as nomads, moving their camel herds and flocks of sheep from oasis to oasis. Many Bedouins have now settled in towns and villages, although they still have a reputation for being independent and hospitable.

Camels are an important part of Bedouin life. Camels are useful as a mode of transportation and a source of food and materials: they can be milked, and their hair made into tents, carpets, and clothes. Bedouin cuisine has been influenced by the limitations of desert life, and lamb and rice form a large part of their diet. Meals are generally eaten in silence, the men dining in a separate tent from the women.

Bedouins may weave rugs or make handicrafts for sale to supplement the family income. Bedouin rugs are woven on small looms and vary between tribes in style and color. Bedouin jewelry is often large and heavy, made from silver or base metal. Finger rings, earrings, and necklaces are favorites.

Over the centuries, Bedouins have become a hardy people, well-adapted to their environment. In the 20th century, however, wars in the Sinai drove many Bedouins to the cities. The Egyptian government is encouraging Bedouins to settle, providing medical services and schools. Some Bedouins have become date farmers; some work on construction projects or in oil fields. Paid employment has changed the way Bedouins live, and cars and trucks are now common features of life in the villages.

NUBIANS

Nubians are people of African descent living in southern Egypt and northern Sudan. They tend to be tall, thin, and dark-skinned, and many Nubian women tattoo decorative patterns on their lips, hands, and feet. There are some 300,000 Nubians. They are mostly Muslim and speak Arabic as well as Nubian.

Traditional Nubian homes are made of clay and straw bricks baked hard in the sun. Both the inside and outside are usually decorated with finger-painted murals of trees and boats.

The construction of the Aswan High Dam flooded the Nubians' centuries-old home along the Nile valley in southern Egypt so that they had to resettle in new areas north of Aswan. Another consequence of the building of the dam was the destruction of ancient Nubian treasures, part of the heritage of today's Nubian people.

The traditional Nubian economy is based on growing date palms, which provide not only food but also timber and rope. Attempts to introduce Nubians to other types of farming have generally not been successful, as they have had little experience outside date farming.

Many Nubians look for work in Egypt's cities. However, family ties remain strong, and they usually return to their home village when they have earned enough money in the city.

Like Bedouins, Nubians are known for their hospitality, which tourists can get a taste of during guided tours into Nubian villages.

Nubians shop at a local market near Kôm Ombo, a resettlement area.

Students in an oasis town wait for class to start.

PEOPLE OF THE OASES

Egyptians who live in the oases are originally of Amazigh descent, with many later influences. Many who live in Kharijah oasis, on the great caravan route, have dark skin, owing to their African ancestry. Whatever their ethnic mix, however, the oasis dwellers tend to see themselves as culturally different from Egyptians who live along the Nile.

The oases are blue-and-green havens in the vast desert. They are known for their natural springs, date palms and other fruit trees, and ancient ruins. The pace of change in the oases is somewhat slower than it is along the Nile, although paved roads are gradually exposing some oasis communities to modern influences such as tourism. Oases in the Western Desert include Dakhla, Farâfra, Khârga, and Siwa.

In the remote Siwa oasis, there are significant differences in customs, clothing, and language. Siwa has a population of some 10,000, and the people are a mixture of Amazigh, Bedouin, and Sudanese. Siwa women lead very restricted lives. They generally cover themselves from head to foot with a square grey woolen cloth when they are outside the home, if they are allowed to leave at all.

PEOPLE OF THE EASTERN DESERT

Two peoples, the Ababdah and the Bisharin, survive in the harsh natural environment of the Eastern Desert. These two groups belong to a larger group of people known as the Beja, who live between the Nile valley and the Red Sea, as far south as Ethiopia.

The Ababdah live in the area immediately south of Aswan, while the Bisharin occupy the southwestern corner of Egypt, extending into the Sudan. Both groups speak a language called *To Bedawi* (TOW BAY-dah-wee), although most Ababdah and some Bisharin men also know Arabic.

The Ababdah and the Bisharin tend to be small and muscular in build and have a dark complexion. The women wear gold or silver jewelry and wrap themselves in colorful cloth. The men hang charms around their necks and wear daggers attached by leather straps to their arms.

Some members of both groups still live their traditional nomadic life in the inner desert; they call themselves the Mountain People. They take shelter from the elements in small cocoon-shaped dwellings made from tree branches and covered with rugs. These dwellings can be quickly packed and carried to a new spot whenever the group moves in search of food and water.

Few people anywhere else on the planet live in as much isolation from the rest of the world as do the Mountain People. The only outside contact they have is with former nomads who have settled in communities on the edge of the Eastern Desert. The Mountain People trade with these settlers, bringing their animals to the markets and exchanging them for sugar, coffee, flour, gold, and silver.

Most of the sedentary population of the Eastern desert live in settlements, trading or herding goats, camels, and sheep for a living.

POPULATION CONTROL

Already one of the most populous countries in the Middle East, Egypt is still seeing very rapid population growth—some 1.5 million people are added to the population every year. This puts a tremendous strain on Egypt's limited resources.

Lacking arable land to substantially increase agricultural output, Egypt will have to import even more food in order to feed its rapidly growing population. And as more young Egyptians enter the labor market, many have to leave the rural areas to look for work in the cities. This breaks up traditional rural family ties and strains urban infrastructure. Housing, medical systems, education, and transportation in the cities are struggling to meet rising demands, while the lack of job opportunities in Egypt drives many skilled workers abroad.

High infant mortality rates moderated the effect of high birth rates in the past, but improvements in medicine and healthcare have eradicated many endemic diseases. Since the 1960s, the government has been

THE GALABIA

In Egyptian villages, the most common dress for men is the *galabia* (GEH-lah-bia), which resembles an ankle-length nightshirt. It has long, loose sleeves and a round neck. The winter *galabia* is made from flannel or heavy cotton; the summer version is lighter. *Galabia* generally come in dull colors. The *galabia*, while very much an Egyptian dress, is generally used by other people in the Middle East as well, although in modified designs, such as the Saudia and Quait.

Underneath the *galabia*, Egyptian men wear cotton shirts and shorts. They may take off the *galabia* when working outdoors, in the fields. Some men, particularly the older ones, also wear a woolen skull cap.

Egyptian women traditionally wear a black dress similar to a *galabia*. They also wear a head covering and sometimes a face veil. Some of the younger women prefer a long cotton dress with bright patterns.

promoting family planning programs. There has been some success, especially among the urban middle class. The fertility rate has fallen in recent decades to around three children per woman in 2002, and the government aims to further reduce this rate in 15 years to around two children per woman. Government expenditure on family planning will have to increase dramatically, and support from foreign donors such as USAID will be crucial.

LIFESTYLE

EGYPTIANS IN THE CITIES have vastly different lifestyles from those in the countryside. Villagers still tend to live in close, change-resistant communities. Rural life is dominated by the daily routine of tending the crops and livestock. The greatest change to the lifestyle of rural Egyptians has been the migration of an increasing number of young adults to the cities in the hope of finding jobs.

Egyptians living in the cities, especially those who are educated or wealthy, live a far more cosmopolitan life. Although urban entertainment, fashion, and food have been influenced by the West, religious (Islamic) beliefs and traditions remain the unifying factor that distinguishes the Egyptian lifestyle.

Left: **A busy scene in Cairo.**

Opposite: **Egyptians relax outside an eating place in the city to enjoy the cooler night air over drinks with friends.**

CHILDREN

Egyptians love children, and a big family is considered a blessing from God. In the past, there were very practical reasons for having a large number of children. As they grew older they could help with the family's work in the fields, and as adults they could look after their aged parents. Faced with a high infant mortality rate, people found it made sense to have as many children as possible in order to increase the probability of at least some surviving. Although these reasons are losing ground as more Egyptians adapt to urban environments and lifestyles, children continue to be a source of joy for families, even smaller urban families.

Another perceived benefit of raising a big family is linked to a belief among the more traditional men that having many children, especially boys, makes them stronger.

Traditionally, it is the women in the family who take care of the children. The men do not spend as much time with the children as the women do, although the men do fuss over the children when they are together. A father may distance himself even more as the child grows older, sometimes thinking this necessary to maintain the child's respect.

Children in the countryside often have jobs at an early age. Before going to school they look after the family's animals. After school they do their homework, and then they help around the house or with the herd or crops. At harvest time, particularly in the cotton-growing areas of the Nile delta, children work in the fields. Indeed, child labor is a problem in rural Egypt, and many children of poorer families work long hours to supplement the family income.

Attitudes toward children began to change in the 1960s, especially in urban society. Government action to improve the status of children in Egypt includes passing child labor laws that set the minimum age for agricultural employment at 14 years and that restrict the conditions in which children under age 18 can be employed, providing compulsory education for children age 12 and younger, and implementing programs together with child welfare organizations. In addition, poor economic conditions have made people consider whether they have the financial means to support a large number of children.

The Egyptian First Lady, Suzanne Mubarak, has been working to improve the lives of children in Egypt for more than 20 years. She has initiated international conferences to study ways to improve the lives of children in the Middle East. Thanks to efforts by the government and people and institutions concerned for the future of Egypt's children, children in Egypt today have more rights than ever before.

In 1996 the Egyptian government outlawed female circumcision except in cases where the procedure was deemed necessary on medical grounds. However, the tradition persists in the rural areas. The government and NGOs are continuing efforts to educate people and end female circumcision in the country.

CIRCUMCISION

Circumcision was practiced in Egypt as early as during the time of the pharaohs. In Saqqara, the tomb of Ankhmahor, which dates back to the sixth dynasty (2300 B.C.) of the Old Kingdom, is famous for its bas-reliefs that depict the surgical procedure being performed on young Egyptian males.

Today, Egyptian Muslim boys, like Muslim boys in other countries, undergo circumcision in their early years of life. For children who were not circumcised as babies, the circumcision ceremony generally takes place before age five, certainly before puberty. In most cases, the operation is done by a doctor at a clinic.

Circumcision is considered important for personal hygiene, but of greater significance is perhaps its function as a religious rite of passage. The ceremony is a milestone, a reason for feasting and celebrating. In the rural areas, it is customary for a boy on the day of his circumcision to ride a horse around the village, his family and friends following.

Egyptian children attend primary school from ages 6 to 12.

EDUCATION

The Egyptian government provides free compulsory education for children until age 15. After six years of primary school, some children go on to three years of intermediate school and then another three years of secondary school. There are two kinds of secondary school: the general school teaches science, humanities, and mathematics, and awards the General Secondary Education Certificate, the equivalent of the U.S. high-school diploma; the technical school trains students in specialized subjects such as agriculture and industry.

Egyptian students face fierce competition for places at institutions of higher learning. There are 14 public universities, the largest being Cairo University in Giza, and four private universities, such as the American University in Cairo. There are also several specialist institutes that offer courses in drama, ballet, film, and other subjects.

In the past, nearly every Egyptian student hoped to build a career in medicine. However, some of today's top students are opting for other subjects.

Egypt has greatly improved its education system since the revolution, raising the national literacy rate above the 50-percent mark. More than 90 percent of children enroll in school, but many drop out. To encourage attendance, the new school year does not start until after the cotton harvest. In primary school, which is compulsory and free, children study mathematics, science, Islam, and Arabic. The government provides each child with a book for each subject. Students have to take regular exams, and the tests that determine whether they can climb to the next rung of the education ladder are particularly important.

However, despite all the effort the government has put into education, the system is struggling under the pressure of an increasing population. Classes of 45 children are not unusual in government-run schools; neither are dual sessions (morning and afternoon). Also, many teachers tutor privately after a full day at school to supplement their income, as public teaching does not pay well.

Many middle-class Egyptians send their children to private schools, with smaller classes of 30. Before the revolution, there were more than 300 private schools in Egypt, many of which taught in French. Today, there are private schools in the country that teach in French, English, or Arabic.

EGYPTIAN NAMES

Many Egyptians give their children names from the Koran. Muhammad, being the name of the prophet who founded Islam, is by far the most popular boy's name, but other religious names such as Ahmad, Khalid, Mahmoud, Mostafa, Omar, and Osman are also very common among boys. Fatimah and Eisha are examples of widely used religious names for girls.

There was a period after the revolution when the old Arabic names regained their former popularity. Egyptians born during the 1960s and 1970s are more likely to have names such as Wael, Walaa, or Waleed for boys, and Dalia, Liala, or Safa for girls. The trend now, however, is to go back to Koranic names.

Public-school students in Egypt wear uniforms: shirt and trousers for boys; shirt and knee- or ankle-length skirt for girls.

A bride and bridegroom receive well-wishers at their wedding reception at a hotel. Most middle-class Egyptian weddings follow the Western style, with the bride dressed in white and the reception in a five-star hotel.

MARRIAGE

Marriage is a very important part of Egyptian life and is encouraged by the Islamic faith. Marriage is not only the joining of two people but a union between two families that can support each other.

In traditional Islamic society, there was little opportunity for young people to meet, so marriages were arranged by their families. This is still the case in the rural areas, where marriages are not only arranged within the village but are often made between cousins or other relations. Even in middle-class families, parents will probably make a lot of effort to introduce their teenage children to other teenagers who they feel will make good life partners.

There is little opportunity in the countryside for couples who are newly married to own their own home. Instead, the bride starts life with her husband in his family's home, where she is subordinate to both her husband and her mother-in-law until she has children and her status in the family rises.

Marriage

In the cities, however, middle-class newlyweds in particular are no longer willing to live in their parents' home. A man may be expected to provide a furnished home that he can move into with his wife as soon as they marry. This means it could take him several years of earning and saving before he is sufficiently established to attract a bride.

The Egyptian wedding ceremony is very simple, a civil rather than a religious contract. All that is needed is the signing of a formal contract between the bridegroom and the bride's male guardian—usually her father, although it could be her brother or uncle. The contract must be signed in the presence of witnesses. In theory, any respectable Muslim man can act as witness. However, to make the marriage more official, the wedding party visits a special office to acquire the service of a government witness called a *mazoun* (MAA-zoon). The contract usually refers to a sum of money called *mahr* (MAHR), which the groom gives the bride's family to buy furniture before the wedding.

After the service, it is important to announce the marriage, so there is a procession from the house of the bride's family to her new home. In the rural areas, a great feast follows the wedding. Virtually everyone in the village is invited to the feast; even the poorest family will give a big feast, even if it means going into debt to pay for it.

Although Islamic law allows a man to have four wives, it is very unusual in Egypt, where monogamy is encouraged. Generally, a man will only take a second wife if his first wife cannot bear children or becomes ill. Egypt has a very low divorce rate, particularly in the rural areas where it brings shame to both families. When a married couple is facing problems, their relatives try to keep them together. The Koran discourages divorce; Prophet Muhammad described it as "the most hateful of all permitted things." If a woman is widowed, she will often marry a second husband within the same family.

A virtuous wife is a man's best treasure. The most perfect Muslims are those whose disposition is best; and the best of you are they who behave best with their wives. Paradise lies at the feet of mothers.

—A saying attributed to Prophet Muhammad

Egyptian women face great social pressures, but few official restrictions.

THE ROLE OF WOMEN IN SOCIETY

Women in Egypt enjoy greater legal equality with men than do women in many other Arab countries. They do not have to wear veils or traditional Islamic clothing. They vote, go to school, own property, and drive cars.

By Western standards, however, many Egyptian women lead restricted lives. Bearing the main responsibility of raising their children and looking after the home, women are less predisposed to work toward influential positions in society.

The government is trying to promote changes in the status and role of women in Egypt, and today many government organizations employ women as well as men in top management positions. For example, the state-run television and radio stations have both had women managing directors, and Egypt has sent several women ambassadors overseas.

The government can lead the way, but it is difficult to change the centuries-old attitudes of the people. In many households, the woman's place in the home is as restricted as it has always been. It is virtually unheard of for a woman to leave the protection of her family until she is married, and after marriage she is expected to submit to her husband. Single women do not go to the movies without a male family member. Women in the rural areas might never leave the village except to go to the market or a wedding.

Egyptian women have made great gains in education. The percentage of women with a secondary- or university-level education has more than doubled over the past two decades. However, the enrollment rate for girls remains lower than that for boys at all levels. Girls also have a higher

Egyptian women enjoy a bit of leisure time at home.

dropout rate than boys. In many schools, boys are seated nearer the front of the classroom, where they receive more attention. Poorer families are certainly less likely to allow a daughter to go on to higher education.

Although traditional attitudes restrict women in many ways, they also give women certain rights and privileges. Even in the most traditional home, Egyptian women still exert great authority. It is the women who have control over money and legal papers, and who have a great say in the raising of the children.

Perhaps the most important change of all is the opportunity for Egyptian women to limit the size of their families, as the government promotes family planning to control population growth. An increasing number of middle-class women—and even many women in the rural areas—are taking advantage of family planning advice.

A number of NGOs support the cause of women's roles and rights in Egypt. A prominent example is the National Council for Women, which is presided over by the First Lady.

Inside an apartment in Cairo.

THE URBAN MIDDLE CLASS

Today, more Egyptians than ever are living in cities. For the well-to-do, Cairo or Alexandria offers a high standard of living. The Egyptian middle class enjoys many amenities and comforts of modern living. For the not-so-well-to-do, city life offers better job opportunities than in rural areas and the hope of a better lifestyle.

However, city life comes with its own problems. Traffic congestion and pollution affect people's health. There are very few houses in Cairo, so even wealthy families live in apartments. There is no yard, but the apartment is large and comfortable and almost certainly has a balcony where the family can relax. The streets are busy, and children of middle-class families are not likely to be allowed to play outside, so they have to find ways to amuse themselves indoors.

Urban apartments in Egypt are likely to be filled with ornate furniture, and the television is the central feature of the living room. Few Egyptian wives work outside the home; most of them stay home to organize the house and prepare the meals. However, this is changing, as younger women in middle-class families attend college or university.

Most middle-class families employ a maid who lives in the apartment. She looks after the children and does the chores. There may be another family living on the roof, in homemade accommodations. In that case, the family may be employed to keep the stairway tidy and do other small jobs for a small sum of money.

Egypt has a serious urban housing shortage that the government is trying hard to rectify. It is estimated that Cairo's population doubles every 10 years because of the influx of immigrants from the rural areas.

When urban families go out, it is usually to the shopping centers or to visit relatives. Those in Cairo who can afford the high entrance fee to the 614-foot (187-m) Cairo Tower might choose to enjoy a bird's-eye view of the city. After work and school, most families are often content to relax together over a meal and then watch television.

Egyptians can be very enterprising, and sometimes it seems that everybody in Cairo has two or three jobs. Even Egyptians in good occupations often need to have extra sources of income to cover their expenses. An army doctor, for example, may run a private practice in the evenings and may own an extra property in the city that is being rented out. An accountant may do private bookkeeping in the evening, own a share in a relative's shop, and occasionally drive a taxi.

SUPERSTITION

Superstition is deeply ingrained in Egyptian culture. The most common fear is of "the evil eye," which is a spell that brings bad luck. This belief may well relate to the pharaonic story of Horus, who had an eye pulled out in his fight with Seth.

It is believed that the evil eye can cause bad luck or sickness, but there are various ways to ward it off. God's name is often spoken out loud to give protection against bad luck; people may say *Bismillah* (BES-me-lah), which means in the name of God, or *Ma Sha Allah* (MAH-shah-lah), which means what God wills. Such expressions of praise to God show the person's submission to God. People wear these expressions in charms and amulets. Other symbols worn to give protection against the evil eye include a blue bead, an open palm with the fingers spread out, or a representation of an eye.

In the past, infant mortality rates were high in Egypt, and the very young were considered particularly vulnerable to evil spells. Charms, or even a dirty face, were thought to give some protection, as did dressing the child as a sheik or monk, or in cloth begged from others. These practices continue even though infant mortality rates have fallen dramatically.

The evil eye is usually associated with envy, and it is therefore impolite to openly admire someone else's possessions. In the more rural areas, this would be considered quite suspicious behavior. If people believe that they are the victim of a spell, there are several things they can do to break it. For example, they can smash an earthen jar behind the person they believe to be casting the spell. In the case of a spell that has caused illness, a paper doll is pricked with a needle and then burned, and the ashes are moved in circles over the sick person seven times before being thrown away.

Egyptians in the rural areas remain very superstitious, but even in the cities one still sees everyday examples of superstitions. For example, good luck charms dangle from the fenders of many motor vehicles. The charm often takes the form of an old shoe, and losing this talisman is believed to bring extremely bad luck. Many superstitious practices are now performed simply out of habit. Tradesmen or shopkeepers, for example, kiss and touch their forehead with the first piece of money that they receive each day as a sign of thanks and praise to God.

FUNERALS

In Egyptian villages, when a member of the family dies, the women of the household start a ritual wailing. Their cries carry the news of the death to the rest of the village.

In all Islamic lands, the body is usually buried within 24 hours. (This is a sensible practice in countries that are generally very hot.) The corpse is washed, dressed in a shroud, and placed on a bier. The bier is then

carried either to the mosque or directly to the cemetery. All the men of the family take turns carrying the bier, followed by a long procession. It is considered a good deed to join a funeral procession, even if the deceased was a stranger.

At the grave, an imam leads the mourning and recites prayers to God and to the Prophet Muhammad. This is followed by silent prayers and the burial. Muslims do not believe in cremation.

In the home of the deceased, the Koran will be read for several nights and food handed out to the poor. Wealthier families may decide to hold a wake on the evening of the burial. Brightly lit tents are erected for this purpose and gilt saloon chairs hired for the guests. A wake may block a major road, but nobody is likely to show disrespect by complaining.

The mourners are likely to be entertained by a *maqri* (MAH-kri), a professional Koran reader. Some of the more famous readers enjoy a large popular following and have become rich from their performances.

A wake can continue on successive Thursdays after the death, but excessive show of grief may be frowned upon, as it is thought impious to protest the will of God.

RELIGION

EGYPT HAS PASSED through three major religious eras: the ancient Egyptian era, the Christian era, and the Islamic era.

The ancient Egyptians worshiped many gods, such as Re, Hathor, and Anubis. One of the central themes of their religion was a belief in the afterlife, and people went to incredible expense to build tombs to house their bodies after death.

The ancient Egyptian religion proved very resilient and survived well into the Roman period. The Roman emperor, Theodosius I, did not order the old temples closed until the end of the fourth century A.D., and it is probable that the ancient gods continued to be worshiped in secret for some time after that. However, Christianity eventually swept away the Egyptians' ancient beliefs, and for three centuries Egypt was a Christian nation. The Coptic Christians still make up the largest religious minority in Egypt.

In A.D. 639 Arabs conquered Egypt, driven by their new and dynamic religion, Islam. There were considerable social and financial benefits for Muslim converts, and today Egypt is a predominantly Islamic nation. Most Egyptians are Sunni Muslims. Sunni Muslims constitute the majority (about 85 percent) of the world's Muslims.

Unlike some of its neighbors in the region, Egypt has never declared itself an Islamic state. For the past 150 years, Egypt has largely pursued a secular path, respecting Islam but generally separating religion as far as possible from the day-to-day workings of the state. Education is now run by the state rather than the mosques. While Islamic law in principle is the sole source of legislation, Egypt's court system is chiefly secular and applies criminal and civil law based primarily on the French Napoleonic Code. In recent years, however, the influence of conservative Islamists has grown.

Above: **A devout Muslim, spreading his prayer rug, gets ready to pray, facing Mecca.**

Opposite: **Constructed in the Ottoman style in the early- to mid-1800s, the Muhammad Ali Mosque is one of Cairo's outstanding landmarks. It is also known as the Alabaster Mosque.**

ANCIENT GODS

The ancient Egyptians worshiped many gods, who they believed influenced different aspects of everyday life. The gods were portrayed as human, animal, or a combination of both *(below and facing page)*. Many of the gods were local to one town or district, but if the area prospered, the local god would gain wider popularity. (Conversely, if the area faded, so did the local god.) For example, Amon progressed from being the sun god of Thebes to being the king of the gods to being associated with the sun god Re, from which time he became known as Amon-Re.

According to the beliefs of the ancient Egyptians, mummification was necessary to ensure a dead person's entrance to the afterlife. Once the person's soul had passed from the earthly realm it had to wait before the god Osiris and his 42 judges as they weighed the person's heart against a feather. If the scales balanced, the deceased could enter the underworld and enjoy a peaceful afterlife; if the scales tilted, a monster would devour the heart, and the deceased would die a second, permanent death.

Spells, hymns, and prayers written by the ancient scribes were carved on the walls of pyramids from the fifth dynasty onward to help the kings in their journeys in the afterworld. The magical texts later found their way into the tombs of noblemen, and they were eventually compiled into the Book of the Dead, a famous example of which belongs to the royal scribe Ani.

ISIS
Queen of the gods, sister and wife of Osiris. Portrayed as a woman with a throne on her head. Grew popular in the New Kingdom.

RE
Sun god, king of the gods, father of humankind. Shown as a man with a falcon's head and sun disk. Holds an ankh and scepter.

ANUBIS
The embalmer and god of the dead. Shown as a black jackal or a man with a jackal's head.

HATHOR
Goddess of love, birth, and death. Portrayed as a woman with cow's horns and sun disk. Holds an ankh and scepter.

SETH
God of chaos, storms, and the desert. Shown as a man with an animal's head. Murdered his brother, Osiris.

THOTH
Moon god, god of learning, inventor of writing. Shown as a man with the head of an ibis and wearing a crown.

Everything a person needed in the afterlife was placed in the tomb. The pharaohs' tombs had thrones, war chariots, and chambers of gold items. To preserve the dead person's body for the afterlife, its organs were removed and the body dried out and then stuffed with resins and preserving oils, before being wrapped in strips of linen and placed in the tomb.

The ancient Egyptians regarded their kings as divine; the kings were the middlemen between the people and the gods. The pharaohs often associated themselves by name and symbolism with various gods. For example, the name of Seti I (father of Ramses II) is connected to the name of the god Seth, and Amenhotep IV, whose name originally honored the god known as Amen or Amon, called himself Akhenaton in reference to the god Aton.

The pharaohs greatly influenced their religion. For example, the first efforts to organize the many local gods that the Egyptians worshiped into a hierarchy began after Menes united Upper Egypt and Lower Egypt, and the religion was drastically reformed when Akhenaton swept away the old gods in favor of one god. (However, the Egyptians returned to worshiping the old gods after his death, and the priests became more powerful than ever.)

The priests were closest to the pharaohs and had religious power second only to that of the pharaohs. The priests performed religious rituals, read the scrolls to the people, took care of the statues of the gods, and composed magical texts to help people in the afterlife.

NEPHTHYS
Goddess of women, sister of Isis and Osiris, wife of Seth. Depicted with a household object on her head.

HORUS
Son of Isis and Osiris. God of the ruling pharaoh. Portrayed as a man with the head of a falcon and wearing a crown.

OSIRIS
King of the dead. Murdered by his brother, Seth. Resurrected by his wife, Isis.

PTAH
In Memphis, Ptah was believed to be the creator of the world. He was the patron of craftsmen.

SOBEK
God of water, thought to have created the Nile from his sweat. Shown with a crocodile's head.

AMON
King of the gods, patron of the pharaohs. Often identified with the sun god Re, as Amon-Re.

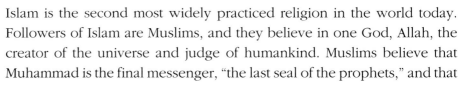

ISLAM

A muezzin summons the faithful to prayer. Traditionally, this is done from a minaret or other part of a mosque at five specified times daily.

Islam is the second most widely practiced religion in the world today. Followers of Islam are Muslims, and they believe in one God, Allah, the creator of the universe and judge of humankind. Muslims believe that Muhammad is the final messenger, "the last seal of the prophets," and that God's revelations to Muhammad complete the series of revelations to Jews and Christians.

The literal meaning of Islam is peace, submitting one's will for God's pleasure. The message of Islam was revealed to Prophet Muhammad 1,400 years ago through the angel Gabriel and was preserved in the Koran. The Koran carries a divine guarantee that safeguards from interpolation and claims to combine the best features of the earlier scriptures.

The prime message of Islam is the unity of God, that the creator of the world is one and he alone is worthy of worship, and that Muhammad is God's messenger and servant. Muslims also believe in the angels, in God's previously revealed books, in all the prophets from Adam to Jesus, in the judgment day, and in God's decree.

Muslims have five main duties: bearing witness to the unity of God and Muhammad as His messenger; observing the prescribed prayers; giving to charity; fasting; and making a hajj, or pilgrimage, to Mecca. Muslims pray five times a day, facing Mecca, at the mosque or wherever they are. Women usually pray at home; when they go to the mosque, they pray

separately from men. Many Egyptians go to the mosque at least for the Friday noon prayer.

The Koran is the sacred scripture of Islam; Muslims believe that the book contains the words of Allah, as revealed to Prophet Muhammad. Many Egyptians have a copy of the Koran at home, probably on a stand, never on the floor. The Koran has 114 chapters, known as *surah* (SOO-rah), each with its own name and varying in length from a few lines to several hundred verses. The language of the Koran is powerful and beautiful, especially when read out loud. The first *surah*, Al-Fatiha, is recited by devout Muslims every day as part of their prayers.

Muslims regard the Koran as the final and complete revelation of God; it cannot be altered. Translations of the Koran are widely available, but they are not used in official ceremonies or in prayers and rituals.

It has been found that the Koran has records of many scientific and technological facts that we have only recently discovered, centuries after the Koran was written. For example, the text of the Koran accurately describes astronomical facts such as the shape of the earth and the orbit of the planets and natural phenomena such as fetal composition and human growth phases.

Muslims pray at dawn, mid-day, mid-afternoon, sunset, and evening. They wash their hands, mouth, face, and feet before praying. When praying, they bow, prostrate, and recite prayers.

An Islamic lecture at the Al Azhar Mosque, which was founded in A.D. 972 by the Fatimids.

THE IMAM Any Muslim man of good faith can lead the prayers at the mosque. (Islam emphasizes closeness to God.) A woman may lead the prayers only if there are no men in the congregation.

Besides leading the prayers, the imam might give lessons in the Koran and answer people's questions regarding the interpretation of Islamic laws. The imam is also expected to give a sermon on Friday after the prayers. This gives him considerable influence over his community, and most mosques appoint a trained imam. The Al Azhar Mosque, located in Cairo, has been a training center for teachers, missionaries, and religious judges for centuries and is today a university for religious studies.

The government approves major religious appointments and controls who is allowed to give sermons on television and radio. An imam who has a reputation as a dynamic or controversial speaker can draw thousands of people to the mosque. Popular sermons are recorded for sale and in this way reach a larger audience.

THE HAJJ

It is the duty of every Muslim to visit the holy city of Mecca at least once in his or her life, unless prevented from doing so by poverty or illness. Every year, thousands of Egyptians make the hajj, and when they return to their villages many pilgrims paint murals on the outside of their houses, showing scenes from their journeys (*below*). Apart from religious rituals, many of these murals include pictures of aircraft or passenger ferries, a reminder that for many Egyptians the hajj may be the only chance they will ever get to see the outside world.

The hajj is performed during the second week of the 12th month of the Islamic calendar. At the start of the hajj, male pilgrims put on an *ihram* (EE-rahm), which is made from two white sheets of seamless cloth. This symbolizes purity and makes all people equal, whatever their status or wealth. There is no prescribed dress for women, but they must go veiled.

The pilgrims enter the *haram* (HAH-rahm), the sacred area around Mecca that is forbidden to non-Muslims. At the Great Mosque, Muslims walk seven times around the Ka'bah, a 40-foot (12-m) long, 50-foot (15-m) high block of black granite that is the central shrine of Islam all Muslims face when praying. Muslims believe that the Ka'bah marks the place where heavenly bliss and power directly touch the earth.

The pilgrims now perform the *sa'y* (sah-EE), a ritual that involves running seven times between the hills of Safa and Marwah. Then the hajj moves to Mina, some 5 miles (8 km) east, for a time of prayer and meditation. Starting when the sun passes the meridian, the pilgrims stand and pray on the plain of Arafat, where Muhammad preached his last sermon. The afternoon of prayer and meditation, which continues until just before sunset, is considered the supreme experience of the pilgrimage to Mecca.

The pilgrims spend the night at Muzdalifah and then go back to Mina just before daybreak. They spend three days at Mina, throwing seven stones at each of three pillars each day. The throwing of the stones symbolizes the casting out of evil.

At the end of the hajj, the pilgrims sacrifice an animal as a gesture of renunciation and thanksgiving, and then they distribute the meat to the poor.

A Coptic priest conducts a service, the Cross of Saint Mark in his right hand.

CHRISTIANITY

The Coptic Christians are the largest religious minority in Egypt. There is a particularly large concentration of Coptic Christians in central Egypt, around the city of Asyut. There are also large Coptic communities in Luxor, Cairo, and Alexandria. An official estimate puts the number of Christians in Egypt at just over two million, although the church claims that the figure is really around five million.

It is widely believed that Saint Mark brought Christianity to Egypt in the first century A.D. Persecuted by the Romans, many Christians sought refuge on the edge of the desert, where they lived as hermits. Later, they formed small religious communities. This monastic life is still an important part of Coptic Christianity today, and there are several large, active monasteries in Egypt, such as Saint Anthony's in the Arabian Desert near the Red Sea.

Christianity began to prosper in Egypt after it became the religion of the Roman empire, and the Greek Church was soon ruling over 40 bishoprics in northern Egypt.

In A.D. 451 the Greek Church broke away from the Church of Rome over the issue of Monophysitism: the Church of Egypt retained the belief that Jesus had a single, divine nature; the Church of Rome took the belief that Jesus was both divine and human.

This difference still separates the Egyptian Coptic Church from the Roman Catholic Church.

Today Coptic Christianity has its own leader, or pope; the current Coptic pope is Shenouda III. Outnumbered by Muslims, Copts tend to maintain tight communities. In the past, they established their own schools, which today are open to anyone and may have many Muslim pupils. The Egyptian government has a policy of tolerance toward Christians, and there have been Christians in high office.

There are also Catholics and Protestants in Egypt, and they have their own churches. Sunday, the main religious day for Christians, is a work day in Egypt. So Christians are allowed time off from work on Sunday to go to church. Churches normally have two services, one in the morning and one in the evening.

Music forms an important part of church services, and there are hymns in Arabic (the official language of Egypt) as well as in Coptic (the traditional language of the Copts). Coptic church services are the only opportunity for the use of the Coptic language in Egypt today.

An entrance to a Coptic church in Egypt.

SAINT MARK

Saint Mark, the most important saint of the Copts, was one of the chief figures in early Christianity. He accompanied Saint Paul on his first missionary journey and traveled to Crete with his cousin Saint Barnabas.

According to Christian tradition, Saint Mark was the author of the second Gospel and the founder of the church in Alexandria. He is believed to have died a martyr's death.

LANGUAGE

THE NATIONAL LANGUAGE of Egypt is Arabic. It originated in the Arabian Peninsula before the birth of Islam. Arabic is classified as a Semitic language, and this puts it in the same group of languages as Hebrew and Ethiopic. It is probable that Arabic script evolved from a dialect of Aramaic, the ancestor of many Middle Eastern and Asian languages.

Arabic spread in the Middle East as Arab armies swept through the region in the seventh and eighth centuries A.D. Arabic has become one of the world's major languages; it is the official language of 17 countries and is spoken by more than 120 million people. It is also the language of the Koran and therefore has religious significance to millions of non-native Arabic speakers.

Arabic writing uses 28 symbols and is read from right to left and from top to bottom. Many of the letters are flowing and circular and look very attractive. There has been a long tradition of competitions where sections of the Koran are copied out, so handwriting has become a respected art form. Indeed, the word calligraphy comes from Arabic and means the art of handwriting.

There are many different scripts. Originally, the Kufic script that developed in the Iraqi city of Kufah was the most widely used. However, a relatively plainer script called Naskhi gained popularity. Today Naskhi is the main script used because it is very clear and ideal for modern printing. Other scripts are used for different purposes. Official documents may be printed in Diwani or Diwani Jali, both very ornate, formal scripts, which were brought to Egypt by the Ottoman Turks.

Above: **An Egyptian reads the *al-Ahram*, the best-known daily newspaper in Egypt.**

Opposite: **A colorful banner in Arabic stretches below a Pepsi billboard in Luxor.**

87

DIFFERENT FORMS OF ARABIC

There are many different written and spoken forms of Arabic. Classical Arabic, the language of the Koran, is described as a written language, although it may be used in speech, such as in sermons and plays. Novels written in a more modern form of Arabic may also use classical Arabic to record dialogue between characters.

Colloquial Arabic is significantly different from classical Arabic. There are nine major regional dialects, which differ in vocabulary, grammar, pronunciation, and syntax. Someone from Lebanon or Iraq may have difficulty understanding an Egyptian. Indeed, northern Egyptian and southern Egyptian are two separate and distinct dialects. Two Egyptians meeting for the first time would be able to tell whether the other is from Cairo or upper Egypt by the way they speak, although they would have no problem understanding each other.

Because of these regional differences, Egypt has been developing a third form of Arabic that is simpler than classical Arabic and that avoids the problems of colloquial Arabic. This third form, sometimes called modern standard Arabic, is understood throughout the Arab world and is used by the leaders of different Arab nations whenever they meet. Its written form appears in newspapers, formal documents, and works of nonfiction, while its spoken form is increasingly heard on radio and television and in formal speeches.

Modern literary Arabic has always used the Koran as a guide and has thus stayed quite close to classical Arabic. Modern Arabic is more similar to classical Arabic than many other present-day languages are to their predecessors. So Arabs today would probably have less trouble reading an ancient classical manuscript than English-speakers might have understanding a novel written in middle English.

Below: **"In the name of Allah, the Compassionate, the Merciful" in Arabic calligraphic script, which has its origin in the days when it was used to beautify the Koranic text.**

Opposite: **Two Egyptians in lively conversation.**

COLORFUL EXPRESSIONS

Arabic is a colorful and expressive language. Daily conversations are filled with popular expressions, many with a religious meaning, that communicate a sense of gratitude and generosity. For example, *al Hamdulillah* (al HAHM-du-lee-lah) means praise be to God, as in "Our plane arrived safely in Cairo, *al Hamdulillah*;" while *insha Allah* (een-SHAH AWL-lah) means if God wills it, as in "My car will be ready tomorrow, *insha Allah*."

If a driver crashes into a wall and gets out safely, he or she will say *Maalehsh* (MAH-lesh), which means it doesn't matter, too bad, or don't take it seriously. This is partly to save face, but it also acknowledges that things could have been worse.

Egyptians have other colorful expressions for greetings as well. For example, when someone wishes another person "Good morning," he or she may be wished back "Morning of light." The first person may then reply "Morning of jasmine," and this will probably be followed by a series of questions about each other's health and family. But no matter what the truth may be, it is customary to say that everything is wonderful—ending every statement with *al Hamdulillah*.

SPEAKING WITH THE REST OF THE WORLD

Arabic does not translate particularly well into other languages. Since it uses a unique script and alphabet, there are often disagreements about how certain words should be spelled. So when naming Egyptian people and cities using the Roman alphabet, print media have to choose one of two or more possible spellings for the same Arabic name. For example, Asyut can also be spelled Assiut, Fayyoum and Fayyum are one place, and the soccer player El Khatib may find his name spelled Al Khatib.

One source of confusion is the absence of many Arabic letter sounds in spoken English. For example, some Arabic letters indicate a strong guttural sound. Different systems of translation use different letters, combinations of letters, and punctuation and accent marks to represent Arabic letter sounds in the Roman rendering.

Generally, provided the text you are referring to uses the accepted spelling for Arabic words, if you see the letter *k*, it probably sounds like "k" in English, while the letter *q* may sound either like "k" at the back of the throat or like "g," or it may be a silent letter. A combination of *g* and *h* (*gh*) may sound like "r" in French.

Translation becomes even trickier when one considers the fact that the regional dialects may pronounce the same Arabic letter differently. Also, Arabic letters are mostly consonants; there are hardly any symbols to represent vowel sounds in written Arabic.

Learning a foreign language is becoming increasingly important for young Egyptians. Traditionally, wealthy Egyptians would learn French; but today English is considered the most important language to know. Recognizing the importance of foreign language skills in opening up career opportunities in other countries, university students take some of their courses in English or French, rather than in Arabic.

Egypt's continuing efforts to speak with the rest of the world is vividly reflected in the state-of-the-art Bibliotheca Alexandrina, which has a wall etched with alphabets from nations both ancient and modern.

ARABIC WORDS IN ENGLISH

During the early spread of Islam, the Arab people were a dynamic force. Apart from being a great military power, they led the world in trade, science, and navigation. Just as today we see English giving the whole world a computer vocabulary, so 800 years ago did Arabic lend many words to other languages.

From Arab astronomers we have adopted the names of many stars, such as Altair, Algol, and Aldebran.

From Arab traders we borrowed the words satin, cotton, sequin, tariff, checks, saffron, and caraway.

Arab mathematicians gave us the words algebra and average.

And Arab chemists gave the world words such as alcohol and alkali.

Egyptian hieroglyphs incised in stone. The written language of the ancient Egyptians consisted of 750 signs. Most were pictures of people, animals, plants, or other objects.

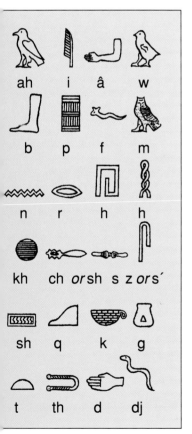

ah	i	â	w
b	p	f	m
n	r	h	h
kh	ch or sh	s z	or s′
sh	q	k	g
t	th	d	dj

THE LANGUAGE OF THE ANCIENT EGYPTIANS

Egyptian hieroglyphs (or the Egyptian hieroglyphic writing system) first developed around 3000 B.C., with symbols to represent objects and actions. The word hieroglyph means sacred carvings. The ancient Egyptians called hieroglyphs the words of the gods. Some hieroglyphs represent sounds; others represent concepts. Eventually more than 5,000 signs were created, although many were only occasionally used. The size of the hieroglyphic vocabulary made the language very difficult to master, and over time its use became limited to carvings on monumental tomb and temple walls.

In addition to hieroglyphs, a cursive form of writing known as Hieratic was used by the ancient Egyptian scribes. Its signs are derived from hieroglyphic counterparts, but are more simplified and much quicker to write. Around the seventh century B.C., a new form of writing emerged. This script is known as demotic and was an even more cursive and abbreviated writing style. However, the Egyptians continued using

THE ANCIENT EGYPTIAN PUZZLE

Much of ancient Egypt was still a mystery before the 19th century. There was a whole world of information carved on tomb walls or written on papyrus, but this was in a forgotten language that no living person understood. Most of our written information came from the early Greek travelers, whose notes and books people could still read and translate. However, there was only a tiny amount of such information, which had been written long after the ancient Egyptian civilization had gone into decline. The secrets of ancient Egypt remained out of reach.

Then in 1799 an officer in Napoleon Bonaparte's army made a wonderful discovery outside the town of Rosetta. It was a slab of black stone that had three types of writing carved into it: the first two were the ancient Egyptian scripts, hieroglyphic and demotic; but the third was Greek, a language people still understood.

For the first time in history, scholars had a key to unlock the written treasures of ancient Egypt. However, the task was not easy—imagine having one page of a book in English and a copy of the same page in French, and having to teach yourself French from that.

The man credited with breaking this ancient code is Jean François Champollion. He was a genius, who at age 11 had taught himself most of the European languages. At 18 he was a professor of history at Grenoble University. The Rosetta Stone became his great challenge.

By comparing the Greek with the Egyptian text, he worked out some of the meanings and sounds of the ancient language. He also understood Coptic, a language related to the earlier demotic and hieroglyphic languages, and this knowledge enabled him to decipher other words.

However, it was not until 1822 that Champollion managed to translate the complete text and publish his findings in a monograph, *Lettre à M. Dacier*, which finally unlocked the lost world of ancient Egypt for modern peoples to explore.

The Rosetta Stone was an incredible find, and nothing similar has since been discovered. The stone is one of many Egyptian treasures in foreign museums. People wishing to see it have to visit the British Museum in London, although there is a copy in Cairo.

hieroglyphs for important religious inscriptions until around A.D. 400. The use of hieroglyphs died out during the later part of Roman rule.

The ancient scribes belonged to a very honored profession, and the wealthy sent their sons to school to learn the written language. Students spent hours copying out hieroglyphs on papyrus, using pens made from reeds and ink made from a mixture of soot and water.

ARTS

EGYPT HAS A LONG ARTISTIC TRADITION. The ancient Egyptians transformed everyday items and translated figments of the imagination into works of beauty. With great vision and precision, they shaped and textured interesting yet practical pots and jars, sculpted grand images of the gods, decorated pyramids and coffins with meaningful symbols, and designed elaborate jewelry using precious stones and metals.

The arts remain an important part of Egyptian culture today. Over the last 150 years, however, Egyptian art has been greatly influenced by the Western world, as modern Egyptian painters, novelists, musicians, and filmmakers combine Western styles with ideas and emotions from their own experiences and culture.

ANCIENT LITERATURE

Probably only about 2 to 5 percent of Egyptians were literate during pharaonic times. Yet Egypt had a rich literary scene during the Middle Kingdom (1980–1630 B.C.), considered the classical era of ancient Egyptian literature: poems, songs, stories, and instructional texts on a range of subjects, such as magic, mathematics, medicine, and astronomy.

Above: **Ancient Egyptian carvings continue to inspire artists in modern Egypt.**

Opposite: **A curios seller in Cairo.**

Much of ancient Egypt's poetry was religious, some similar in style to the psalms in the Bible. There were complex stories with gods and goddesses, and various genres were found in some texts.

The ancient writers used puns, similes, and metaphors, and paid attention to presentation as well. Ancient Egyptian script was normally written from right to left, but for artistic purposes it could also be written from left to right or from top to bottom.

Writers such as Taha Hussein and Naguib Mahfouz have brought Egyptian literature to the world's attention. Many of their works have been translated and published in other languages.

MODERN LITERARY FORMS

Under the influence of Arabic, folktales and narrative essays called *makama* (MEKH-ah-mah) became popular. However, poems retained their importance, as they were written for the common people. One of Egypt's best-known poets was Amal Dunqul (1940–83), whose works focused on his country's political experience and connected with the sentiments of the nation, especially in the 1960s and 1970s.

Magazines are widely read in Egypt, and short stories are an effective way for writers to reach a large audience. Many writers have also turned their attention to novels, adapting this Western concept to develop their own storywriting style. Some of the earliest Egyptian novels looked at Western influences on Egypt. Tawfiq al-Hakim's *The Bird from the East* and Yahya Haqqi's *The Lamp of Umm Hashim* are good examples.

One of the earliest important books to look at life in the Egyptian countryside was Muhammad Husayan Haykal's *Zaynab*. Taha Hussein

NAGUIB MAHFOUZ—NOBEL PRIZE WINNER

Egyptian writing caught the world's attention in a big way in 1988 when Naguib Mahfouz received the Nobel Prize for literature.

Born in 1912, Mahfouz was the son of a minor government official. There were no Egyptian novels while he was growing up, and he found inspiration in the works of European writers such as Tolstoy and Proust. Mahfouz studied philosophy at the Cairo University and then entered the university administration.

Mahfouz's first novels were set in pharaonic times, but he became famous for his stories of Cairo's bazaars and alleyways. Besides his most famous book, *Midaq Alley,* he has written *The Cairo Trilogy,* which names the streets and squares of Old Cairo—*Palace of Longing, Between Two Palaces,* and *The Sugar Alley.* In the books, Mahfouz traces the life of a merchant family from 1919 to 1944, creating wonderful characters and capturing the old city's atmosphere in much the same way that Charles Dickens described Victorian London. Mahfouz also uses the books to examine the hopes and disappointments of the Nationalist Movement. Such works have secured his place as the leading writer of the Arab world.

gained fame with his autobiographical novel, *An Egyptian Childhood.* Born in a village and blind from age three, Hussein nonetheless made outstanding contributions to education and the arts in this country. He obtained not one but two doctorates and worked in high government and university positions.

Egyptian writers cannot survive solely on earnings from their work; they need financial support. There is a limited market for their books at home, and Arabic does not translate easily into other languages. Those who are not granted government support may turn to writing plays or movie scripts instead; or they may write only as a hobby.

However, more Egyptian novels are being translated and exported, following the international success of Egypt's greatest writer, Naguib Mahfouz, who won the Nobel Prize for literature in 1988 for *The Cairo Trilogy.* Another internationally acclaimed author is Nawal El-Saadawi. Her works, including *The Fall of the Iman* (1987), provoked controversy in her home country and have been banned there.

Taha Hussein supervised the translation of the complete works of Shakespeare into Arabic. In 1973 he was awarded the United Nations human rights prize.

MOVIES

Cairo is known as the Hollywood of Arabia, and Egypt produces a thousand or more movies a year for distribution throughout the Middle East. The first movies were being made in Egypt before World War I, but it was the founding of Misr Studios in 1934 that really marked the start of the Egyptian movie industry.

The man who first brought Egyptian movies to a world audience was Yusuf Shahin, who in 1950 directed his first film, *Baba Amin*, at age 24. In 1958 he directed and starred in *Cairo Station*, a film about a street urchin's sexual frustrations, which defined his directorial style. For most of his films, Shahin cast ordinary people from the street rather than big movie stars.

Another great Egyptian director was Alexandria-born Shadi Salam. He learned his art assisting some of the best Egyptian filmmakers of the time. Salam most enjoyed directing films on ancient Egypt—his works include *The Mummy* (1968) and *The Golden Chair of Tutankhamen* (1982).

Cairo has hosted its international film festival annually since 1976. Featuring acclaimed films from around the world, the event is the place to be for the Arab world's filmmakers. Celebrities from Hollywood, California, have also made guest appearances at the Cairo festival. Alexandria hosts its own international film festival as well.

Egypt's cinemas screen both Arabic and subtitled foreign-language films. One Egyptian actor with an international reputation is Michel Shalhoubi, better known as Omar Sharif.

THEATER

Egypt's only traditional theatrical art form is the puppet shadow play. Performers use sticks or strings to move paper or leather puppets behind an illuminated white screen so that the audience sees only the moving shadows of the puppets on the screen.

Puppet shadow plays go back as early as 700 years ago and are still performed in Cairo. They normally consist of just one act, and the puppet characters make lots of (sometimes rude) jokes.

Egypt's simple folk plays originated in the villages, but modern drama is an import. Professional theater in the Middle East started in Syria during the last century.

Cairo is the cultural center of the Arab world. The capital's opera house and its many theaters entertain thousands each year with many excellent productions.

Political persecution by the Turkish authorities forced many troupes to flee to the safety of Cairo. Salim Khalil al-Naqqash was one of these political refugees. In 1878 he wrote *The Tyrant*, the first play ever performed in Arabic. Around that time, Ya'qub ibn Sanu made a major contribution to Cairo theater with his comedies and operettas. He was the first of the early playwrights to use the colloquial dialect rather than classical Arabic.

The best-known of all modern Egyptian playwrights was Tawfiq al-Hakim. As a young man he went to Paris to study law, but spent much of his time in theater and musical performances. When he returned to Egypt, he built a reputation as one of Egypt's most exciting and original writers. He wrote plays such as *The Bargain,* which paid tribute to the Egyptian fellahin. Although he usually wrote in classical Arabic, Hakim often used Egyptian folk dances and songs, which tended to be in colloquial Arabic, to make his work familiar to the common people.

MUSIC AND DANCE

Music and dance were important art forms in ancient Egypt. The early Greek travelers praised the beautiful songs and hymns of the Egyptians. Musical instruments were usually played to accompany the singer's voice and the dancer's movement. The most popular instruments at first were harps and flutes, but the New Kingdom Egyptians either invented or imported lutes and clappers.

A musician in Luxor plays a traditional stringed instrument.

The Arabs brought their own musical instruments, some of which the Egyptians already knew of. The lute became the most important instrument, although the viola, tambourine, and drum, and a fiddle called *rabab* (rahb-EUB) were also used. Sports and the fine arts received little attention from the Arabs, who developed music into the main art form.

The music of the Arab period can be divided into classical and folk. Classical music was used in the mosques for religious ceremonies and remained strict and formal; folk music was simpler and freer, making it easier to adapt. Both have become familiar to the common Egyptian; a farmer in the fields might sing an age-old folk chant as well as he might a classical piece heard at the mosque.

Like many traditional art forms, both classical Arabic music and folk music in Egypt are under pressure from Western influences. Even villagers have transistor radios, and most Egyptians recognize the sounds of famous American or European musicians. In fact, the best of modern Egyptian music is often considered to be that which combines Western influences with traditional Egyptian sounds. Sayed Darwich, whose work blends classical Arabic music with European opera, is known as the father of modern Egyptian music. Mohammed Abd El Wahab has done a similar job of combining European pop with elements of Egyptian folk music.

The most famous Egyptian singer of all time was Umm Kulthum. More than a vocalist who sang to music played on traditional Egyptian instruments, she was an icon who spoke for Arabic music and musicians and who gave her concert proceeds to her country after it was defeated by Israel in 1967. When she died in 1975, millions of people joined her funeral procession through the streets of Cairo.

Egyptian folk dancers at a local hotel.

Egyptian folk dance is closely linked with traditional Egyptian music. Folk dances were originally developed to celebrate the stages of the agricultural cycle, and they were also performed at weddings or festivals. The dances vary from region to region, with the most distinctive ones coming from the far south and the oasis regions.

Egypt is also famous for belly dancing. The belly dance originated in Turkey but is enjoyed by many Egyptians. There are several versions of the dance. Belly dancers may, for instance, hold candles in their hands or fasten candles to their headdress, so that the candlelight emphasizes the grace of the dance.

Ballet in Egypt is influenced by the famous Bolshoi Ballet. The Cairo Opera Ballet Company was founded in 1966, and original ballets by Egyptians include *Steadfastness*, which was inspired by the 1967 war.

MODERN ART

Arabs have little tradition for the fine arts. However, there is an Egyptian School of Fine Arts, and the government encourages fine arts exhibitions and competitions.

Mahmoud Mokhtar (1891–1934) is the best-known modern Egyptian artist; many of his imaginative sculptures are displayed in his own museum in Cairo. One of the women pioneers of the modern art movement was Inji Aflatoun (1924–89).

The Egyptian Museum of Modern Art in Cairo displays the works of Egyptian artists from the 20th and 21st centuries.

The Wisa Wassef weaving school produces some exciting tapestry. The founder, Ramses Wisa Wassef, began with an isolated group of Harraniyyah villagers, who got their ideas and inspiration from their environment. Animals and landscapes feature in nearly all the Wisa Wassef tapestries. Each piece may take months to complete, and the colors and style often reflect the mood of the artist.

The second generation of Wisa Wassef weavers is producing highly prized works. Wisa Wassef tapestries hang in some of the greatest museums in the world, and kings and millionaires have visited the workshops.

FOLK ART

Egypt has a wealth of folk art. For centuries, artists have made everyday objects decorative, partly to make them pleasing to the eye, but also to turn then into investments.

The traditional materials used by folk artists are brass, copper, ivory, silver, and gold. Wood is seldom used, simply because Egypt does not have any forests.

Cottage industries flourish, and artisans use traditional skills passed down through generations to transform raw materials into works of art.

Above: **A brilliantly colored woven rug conveys scenes of rural life.**

Opposite: **Putting pen to paper to produce a carpet design.**

COPPER AND BRASS   Although the sheets of metal are now produced in factories, copper and brass objects are still hammered out by hand in small family workshops. Mirror frames, trays, plates, vases, coffee pots, and smoking pipes are the most common objects manufactured. Tourist souvenirs such as name plates and Christmas tree ornaments are also being produced.

When damp, copper becomes toxic, so an item intended to be used in cooking should be lined with tin or silver. To make the metal more durable and easy to work with, it is often mixed with other metals. Brass, a common working metal, is a combination of copper and zinc. It has a golden color that makes it popular for decorative pieces.

To make the items more attractive, they might be embossed, chased, or inlaid.

INLAID WORK   Wooden chessboards, boxes, and chests are decorated with tiny pieces of mother-of-pearl laid into the wood to form mosaic patterns. Ivory was also once used for such work, but is now too expensive for most artisans.

JEWELRY   Many Egyptians from the countryside have little knowledge of or faith in banking and prefer to invest in gold or silver. This is kept in the form of jewelry, and has created a whole industry to design and manufacture decorative items. The villagers favor large and bulky items, and this style influences even

modern designs. Earrings, necklaces, and bracelets are the most common pieces. Other influences have come from Arabic calligraphy and tourist demand for pharaonic reproductions.

MASHRABEYYA *Mashrabeyya* (mas-rah-BAY-ah) is the name for Egypt's beautiful wooden latticework windows. They were good for ventilation yet still offered privacy. They became extremely popular in the 19th century, despite the fact that the wood needed to make them had to be imported.

Most of the old *mashrabeyya* windows have been taken to museums, but some shops still practice this old craft. Carpenters today are assisted by a few modern electrical tools.

LEISURE

RELAXING is one of the most popular pastimes in Egypt. The hot desert climate—and manual labor in rural areas—have made people value any free time they can get just to sit somewhere and talk with friends. In the villages, a group of women may gather in the courtyard of one of their homes to chat; most men are likely to spend at least a few evenings in a coffeehouse.

THE COFFEEHOUSE

A typical Egyptian coffeehouse is a large, tiled saloon that is often crowded and alive with activity: coffee bubbling and glasses clinking, waiters squeezing between tables, shoeshine boys hovering, people laughing, dominoes clacking, dice rolling, and cards slapping.

Below: **A group of friends share a smoke in a coffeehouse.**

Opposite: **Riding a felucca is one of the most relaxing pastimes on the Nile.**

Going to a coffeehouse is a social activity, and people usually go with friends. There is a cheerful exchange of news and views among patrons at a coffeehouse, where the country's well-developed art of conversation is put to practice. People are admired for their wit and humor, as they weave proverbs and religious quotations into a discussion of local, national, and international events. In coffeehouses in rural areas, one patron may read aloud from the newspaper to interested listeners.

Many coffeehouses cater to a particular group of people, depending on their location, environment, and service. Some may attract fellahin, others intellectuals; some may be a favorite hangout for young people, others the preferred haunt of retired army officers.

107

THE EGYPTIAN WATER PIPE

The water pipe, also called a hubble-bubble pipe, is the traditional smoking instrument in Egypt and an important part of the ambience and service of any Egyptian coffeehouse.

A water pipe has a glass or brass base that stands on the ground, by the side of the table. The base is filled with water, and tobacco is burned over live coals at the top. The smoker draws the smoke through a 3.3-foot (1-m) soft pipe. But first, the smoke passes through the water, which filters it and lightens its taste. The action produces a gurgling sound in the water that many people find soothing.

Regulars to a particular coffeehouse might keep their own personal pipe there. Many men also enjoy smoking a water pipe at home, and it is often the job of the children to have it ready when their father comes home from work. Egyptian women seldom smoke a water pipe and would certainly not do so in public.

The favorite tobacco, *ma'assil* (MAH-AH-sil), is a sticky blend of chopped leaves fermented with molasses. Dozens of brands of *ma'assil* are sold nationwide, and many local brands are sold within a town or province. Alternatively, smokers might prefer *tumbak* (TOM-bek), which is loose, dry leaves wrapped into a cone.

After some years of declining popularity, the water pipe is once again becoming fashionable, even though, like any form of smoking, it carries serious health hazards. The rising price of cigarettes partly explains the water pipe's return, but many people are turning to the water pipe in an effort to rediscover their own culture.

A NATION OF SPORTS LOVERS

Egyptians love sports and play all the popular games from around the world. Most schools in Egypt have at least a small courtyard, where students play friendly basketball and volleyball matches or train for interschool games. Working adults may engage in sports with friends in their leisure time. Watching competitive games is, of course, a popular alternative to actually playing them.

Egypt's first professional sports were wrestling and weightlifting. At the 1928 Olympics in Amsterdam, weightlifter Nasser El Sayed broke the world record and won Egypt's first ever Olympic title. Egypt continued to bring home Olympic weightlifting medals from Berlin in 1936 and London in 1948, but lost out to other countries in subsequent meets.

The Egyptian men's Olympic swim team is probably Africa's best, especially in long-distance events. Egypt's top swimmers have finished all the great marathon events around the world. Other popular water sports are rowing and sailing. Egyptians sail yachts at al-Maadi, just a few miles south of central Cairo, or in the open sea at Alexandria.

Cyclists all geared up for a ride. Cycling is a popular urban leisure activity.

Egypt also has very good javelin throwers. However, Egyptian track athletes have yet to match the speed and stamina of North African runners, who are ranked among the best in the world.

By African and Middle Eastern standards, Egypt can produce strong teams in hockey, tennis, volleyball, handball, water polo, and basketball, and Egyptian squash players have won world tournaments.

Apart from winning regional events, Egypt has played a leading role in developing sports in Africa and the Middle East. For example, Egypt regularly hosts regional championships. The biggest event in Egypt so far was the 1991 African Games, an Olympic-like meet for teams from all over Africa.

Despite the hot weather, women are expected to keep their legs covered when playing games such as tennis or even when going for a swim at the beach.

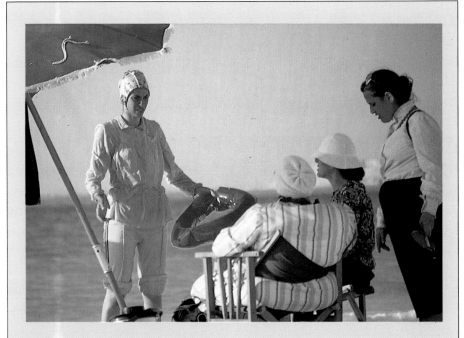

WOMEN AND SPORTS

Egypt sends a large team to the Olympics, but most of these athletes are men. Similarly, although the Egyptian men's teams traditionally do well in the African volleyball and basketball championships, the women's team is never represented in the finals.

Only recently has it become socially acceptable for young women in middle-class families to play sports such as tennis and squash. Girls may enthusiastically practice gymnastics and swimming, and some of the big sports clubs stage "women's only" afternoons in the gymnasium or pool, where women's sportswear can be worn without conflicting with local dress codes.

While women in Egypt are slowly being encouraged to take part in recreational sports, in many parts of the country it is still not considered normal for women to take sports seriously. Egyptian women who train as professional athletes face serious social pressures, such as chauvinistic attitudes, conservative dress codes, and traditional perceptions of gender roles (that women should marry young and start a family). Training for a career in sports may be viewed by society as conflicting with these expected duties and behaviors.

SOCCER: THE GREAT LOVE

Soccer is the undisputed king of Egyptian sports. When a big match is played at the national stadium, the streets of Cairo are deserted, and everyone who is not at the stadium is probably at home, watching the game on television. Fans may react wildly to their favorite team's loss, damaging buildings close to the stadium, and tempers often flare up among the players themselves. However, when the Egyptian national team scores an important victory in an international game, the whole country celebrates, and cars drive around the streets with flag-waving supporters sitting on the roofs.

Soccer was introduced to Egypt by the British. The Egyptians soon learned the game, and by 1907 they had their own club, Al Ahly. The Egyptian Football Association was founded in 1921 to develop soccer in Egypt. In the Olympic tournament in Amsterdam in 1928, Egypt beat Turkey, Portugal, and Argentina to get through the semifinals. The only other time Egypt made it to the semifinals was in 1964 in Tokyo.

Egypt helped to establish a regular soccer meet for African nations during the 1950s, and the African Football Confederation is still based in Cairo. The trophy of the African Nations Cup was donated by an Egyptian army officer, General Abdelaziz Mustapha, and the Egyptian team has won the trophy four times since 1957.

At home, the favorite club is Al Ahly, which nearly always wins the Egyptian league. Zamalek, another Egyptian team (and Al Ahly's great rival), usually puts up a tough fight. Club colors are very important to soccer fans, who often go to matches wearing the same jerseys as the players on their favorite teams. Many Egyptian teams are owned or sponsored by big firms. Arab Contractors, for example, is strongly supported by the Osman group of industrial and engineering companies.

AL AHLY

ZAMALEK

ARAB CONTRACTORS

The united colors of a few Egyptian soccer teams.

FESTIVALS

THERE ARE TWO MAIN TYPES of holidays in Egypt: religious holidays; and national holidays that celebrate important events in Egypt's modern history.

Muslims generally do not celebrate their religious festivals very grandly or colorfully, and there is no reference in the Koran to even the two main religious holidays in Egypt—Eid al-Adha and Eid al-Fitr.

However, since Egyptians love festivals as much as people in any country do, other holidays have been added to the national calendar over the years. The best example is the Prophet Muhammad's birthday. Now an important holiday in Egypt, it was not celebrated until at least 400 years after Muhammad's death.

Above: **Children dress in their best during religious festivals, such as Eid al-Fitr, which celebrates the end of the fasting month.**

Opposite: **Egyptians in Cairo visit the graves of their loved ones during Eid al-Adha, the Feast of the Sacrifice.**

Most Islamic holidays are based on the Hijra (HEZH-rah) calendar. As a result, they are celebrated a little earlier each year compared with the modern Gregorian calendar. Islamic holidays are usually celebrated with extra prayers, sermons, lavish meals, and visits among relatives.

NATIONAL HOLIDAYS

The anniversaries of major post-revolution events give Egyptians more opportunities to get together with their family and friends for a meal. National holidays are marked with special reports and features in the newspapers and on television, and schools and factories may organize formal or social events. Armed Forces Day used to be celebrated with a grand military parade, until President Sadat was assassinated at one. No national parade has been held since, although individual governorates may stage military shows. National Day, on July 23, celebrates the 1952 Revolution and is the most important of the secular holidays.

Egyptians return from abroad on Eid al-Fitr to celebrate the end of Ramadan with their families.

RAMADAN

Observance of the holy month of Ramadan is one of the five pillars of Islam. When Muslims fast, they do not eat or drink while the sun is up. Every day during Ramadan, they fast from sunrise until they hear the prayer call at sunset on the radio or television or from the mosque.

To decide when the day's fast is over, the imam at the mosque holds up two pieces of thread, one white and one black. It is considered night and time to end the fast when he can no longer distinguish between the two colors. The muezzin then announces the end of the fast with a call to prayer. The streets become empty, as people go home to break the fast with their families. They have supper before going to bed, and just before daybreak they wake up for another meal before starting the new day's fast.

Egypt's hot climate makes it particularly difficult to get through the day without refreshment. People often feel very tired during the Ramadan month, and the whole pattern of life changes. Government offices slow down or even stop work altogether, and it is not unusual for office workers to take short naps right at their desks during lunchtime. Schools often close early so that the students can go home for an afternoon nap.

Not everyone has to fast; young children, the sick, and the aged are excused. Travelers, soldiers on duty, and women who are menstruating need not fast during Ramadan, but they should try to make up for "lost" fasting days at a later time.

People are more diligent about saying prayers and reading scripture during Ramadan. Indeed, most families try to read the entire Koran by the end of the month. There is usually a large gathering outside the mosques each evening during Ramadan, as people celebrate the end of another day of fasting. These crowds build up in numbers and excitement as the end of Ramadan approaches.

EID AL-FITR

Eid al-Fitr is the most important holiday in Egypt. It celebrates the end of Ramadan, and in the days leading up to Eid al-Fitr, the airports and harbors are crowded with Egyptians returning from their work abroad to spend the holiday with their families in Egypt.

The end of Ramadan is also the time when Muslims give to the poor a percentage, usually 2.5 percent, of their wealth. This offering is called *zakat* (ZAH-khat), another pillar of Islam. It is considered not as charity, but as an act of worship. Indeed, the name *zakat* means purify, and it reminds everyone that all wealth really belongs to God.

The month of Ramadan ends with the sighting of the new moon. After the end of the fast is announced, the gaiety of Eid al-Fitr begins.

Youths in a festive mood.

EID AL-ADHA

This religious holiday, also known by its Turkish name of Qurban Bairam, marks the end of the holy pilgrimage to Mecca, yet another pillar of Islam.

The main feature of the celebration is the lavish feast. In the days leading up to the festival of Eid al-Adha, everyone who can afford to buys a sheep or goat and leaves the animal in the street outside the house to flaunt the family's wealth and impress the neighbors. The animals are slaughtered on the 70th day after Eid al-Fitr, and big feasts are held at the mosques. A third of the sacrificed animals is given to the poor.

MUHARRAM

Muharram, the Islamic New Year, marks the day Muhammad and his followers set out for Mecca from Medina.

Muharram is New Year's Day for Muslims, but it is not celebrated with big parties the way January 1 is celebrated in the Western world. (However, Egypt does also seem to come to a standstill on the Western New Year's Day, with many people missing work to go out.) Muharram is a festival for the family, as Muslims get together with their families to share a meal and exchange gifts.

The Islamic year has only 354 days, following the lunar calendar. This means that the major festivals occur 12 days earlier each year when compared with the calendar used in the Western world.

COPTIC HOLIDAYS

Coptic celebrations usually take place later in Egypt than in Europe. For example, Christmas is celebrated on January 7. Copts celebrate their religious holidays with church services and family gatherings. They pay particular attention to the saints, and large numbers of people visit once remote monasteries on special saints' days.

An extended Coptic family gathering.

SHAM EL-NESSIM—A LEGACY FROM ANCIENT EGYPT

The legacy of ancient Egypt includes more than their art. Modern Egyptians continue to celebrate a festival that has evolved from the Spring Festival of the ancient Egyptians.

The Spring Festival was the most important festival in ancient Egypt. It celebrated the rebirth of the earth after winter. The day also marked the start of the year, which would run through the agricultural cycle.

During the Spring Festival, people ate eggs, which were seen as a symbol of renewal after death. The practice of eating eggs as a special celebration was adopted by the Jews and Christians. It continues in the Christian world today with the giving of Easter eggs.

The ancient Spring Festival is today known as Sham el-Nessim. This translates from the Arabic as "breathing of the spring air." Sham el-Nessim is a national holiday and is celebrated at the time of the Coptic Easter. Both Copts and Muslims celebrate the holiday, although it is particularly important to Copts.

Sham el-Nessim probably bears little resemblance to celebrations that took place in ancient Egypt, but the eating of eggs has remained a tradition. Ordinary hens' eggs are used, but they are boiled in a coloring to dye them brown. Salted fish and onions are also traditionally eaten on this day and are thought to prevent disease. Many families rise very early to picnic by the Nile or in the countryside.

The ancient Egyptians had numerous other local festivals, such as the Festival of the Living Falcon and the Festival of the Victory of Horus. One of the most important events was the Festival of the Sacred Wedding, when the statue of Hathor was taken from the temple of Dendera and rowed 100 miles (160 km) south to Idfu to meet the statue of Horus (*above*). The festival reenacted the union of Hathor and Horus on the night of the rising of the new moon.

SAINTS' DAYS

In the past, saints' days were occasions for villages to stage elaborate celebrations. Events took place at fairgrounds with bright lights and blaring music, acrobatics, belly dancing, and camel racing. There was also a religious feast at the local mosque.

Saints' days celebrations are now more subdued, and many have died out altogether. The celebrations often led to riots and crime, so the police objected to them. The Islamic authorities supported the suppression of saints' days as such events were considered unorthodox and thought to have pagan links. The only saint's day that is widely celebrated is Mouled al-Nabi (MOO-led ahl-NAH-bee), the birthday of Prophet Muhammad himself. This is an important national holiday, when it is traditional to give children sugar dolls and sweet pastries.

MAIN HOLIDAYS IN EGYPT

ISLAMIC HOLIDAYS

Muharram	New Year's Day
Mouled al-Nabi	Birthday of Prophet Muhammad
Eid al-Fitr	The end of Ramadan
Eid al-Adha	The end of the pilgrimage

COPTIC HOLIDAYS

Christmas	January 7
Epiphany	January 19
Easter	varies
Annunciation	March 21
Feast of Virgin Mary	August 15

NATIONAL HOLIDAYS

New Year's Day	January 1
Sinai Liberation Day	April 25
Evacuation Day	June 18
National Day	July 23
Armed Forces Day	October 6

OTHER HOLIDAYS

Sham el-Nessim	varies

FOOD

EATING IN EGYPT is often a social event. Be it at a family gathering or a business meeting, a meal may consist of several courses and cups of coffee. Often the food takes second place to the conversation.

DAILY MEALS

Egyptians may have as many as five meals a day. Breakfast, at least in the city, is usually a drink at home and some *foul* (fool)—a bean dish—and bread bought from a stall on the way to work. By mid-morning, most Egyptians will have had a light meal of bread with cold meats, pickles, or eggs, and coffee or tea.

For lunch, people in the rural areas might have bread, cheese, dates, and vegetables; meat and fish, which are more expensive than vegetables, are reserved for special occasions. There are several kinds of Egyptian cheese: soft, hard, pickled, and spicy. People in the cities can also choose from a variety of Western cheeses.

For people in the cities, lunch may consist of rice, a meat dish, and a salad. Bread and rice are the main staples in Egypt. Yellow saffron rice with boiled lamb is a typical main course, while rice boiled with milk and sugar makes a popular pudding for dessert.

The evening meal, usually eaten at home, may be rice with cooked meats and vegetables. There will also be bread and perhaps olives and salads. Poorer families may simply have bread and stew. Fresh fruit, especially red watermelon, is a popular way to close any meal.

A typical supper, eaten at around 10 o'clock, consists of *foul* with perhaps fried vegetable balls or grape leaves stuffed with rice.

Above: **Tamia, a popular Egyptian meal of ground beans and green vegetables fried in oil and served with tomatoes, lemons, and eggplant.**

Opposite: **A woman in Cairo making traditional bread.**

COMMON INGREDIENTS

Even the wealthiest in Cairo use the same ingredients in many of their meals as do people in the poorer areas. Generally, Egyptians use fresh ingredients when cooking.

Olive oil is used mainly for cooking, but it may also be mixed with spices and nuts to make a spread. Olives are a favorite, seldom used as a cooking ingredient but often served as a snack with bread and cheese. The most common Egyptian cheese, a soft white cheese similar to feta, is made from sheep's or goat's milk.

A good Egyptian cook uses a variety of spices, such as camphor, caraway seeds, cumin, marjoram, myrrh, saffron, and thyme, to season anything from vegetable soups to meat kebabs. Egypt is located on the

FOUL MIDAMMIS (FOOL MEE-DAH-MESS)

6 1/2 ounces (184 g) dried fava or broad beans
1/2 ounce (14 g) dried red lentils
3 cups water
3 tablespoons olive oil
2 1/2 teaspoons lemon juice
1/2 teaspoon salt
1 tablespoon chopped fresh parsley
Black olives (optional)

Wash the beans and lentils in a colander, then drain thoroughly. Boil the water. Add the beans and lentils, then lower the heat. Partially cover, and simmer for three to four hours, adding more boiling water if necessary. There should be almost no liquid left when the beans are done. Remove from the heat to cool. Mix the olive oil, lemon juice, and salt in a large bowl. Add the beans and lentils, then mash until the beans absorb the liquid. Garnish with parsley and olives.

Sacks full of dried herbs and spices in a market.

traditional spice route between Asia and Europe, and today many towns in Egypt have entire markets that sell nothing but spices.

Certain vegetables feature more prominently in Egyptian cuisine than in Western cooking, eggplant perhaps being the best example. Brought from India more than 1,500 years ago, this dark purple vegetable also known as aubergine has found its way into many Egyptian recipes. Eggplant may be used to make a dip such as *baba ghannooj* (bah-bah GAH-nooj), or baked with grilled lamb or mutton to make *moussaka* (MOO-sah-kah).

Other common vegetables in Egypt include cauliflower, cucumber, onion, spinach, and tomato. The green pods of the okra plant often form the base of stews and soups.

Fava beans are used to make *foul*. They may be boiled, then pureed with onions and spices; or mashed with different spices and shaped into patties and deepfried. Chickpeas are mixed with lemon juice, olive oil, and various spices to make hummus, eaten with pita bread.

Wheat, widely grown in Egypt, is used in baking bread. Corn is the popular staple for the peasants.

FOOD IN ANCIENT EGYPT

Thanks to the fertile waters of the Nile, the ancient Egyptians enjoyed a variety and abundance of food that would have been the envy of other early civilizations. Although there was always the danger of floods and famine, in good years Egypt was a land of plenty.

Many of the foods that the ancient Egyptians ate were the predecessors of foods that people living along the Nile today still enjoy. Then, as now, bread was probably the staple food; indeed, the ancient Egyptians were among the first people to learn how to make leavened bread. They had many different bread recipes, some flavored with spices or with fruit such as dates. The ancient Egyptians also discovered the art of brewing; they made beer from barley, wheat, or dates. Beer was consumed with most meals, perhaps because ordinary water was considered unsafe.

The ancient Egyptian gardens grew a wide variety of produce, including cabbages, celery, grapes, and onions. People cooked lentils in soups and stews, while poultry and fish were important parts of the diet. Cattle, oxen, and sheep were kept for meat and milk.

Cooking was done in mud ovens and roast pits, or over open fires. Tableware was made from clay, and the rich had drinking cups made from metal. There were spoons and knives, but much of the food would have been eaten with the fingers.

Selection and preparation were very important processes in dealing with food. Food had more than dietary uses; it was also offered for the dead. Indeed, much of our information about diet in ancient Egypt comes from drawings in tombs. For example, there are images of great feasts where a whole ox was roasted. Since the royal tombs were given far more attention, today we have very little information about the food that the poor of ancient Egypt ate.

INFLUENCES OF OTHER CUISINES

Egyptian cuisine reflects a Turkish influence, part of the legacy of the Ottoman empire, of which Egypt was a part for several hundred years. *Kebab* (KAY-bahb) and *moussaka*, for example, are basically the same in Egypt as in other countries around the eastern Mediterranean.

Egypt has inherited culinary influences from its other foreign rulers as well, and many Egyptian dishes have Greek or Syrian roots.

In recent times, Egyptian food, especially in the cities, has also come under international influence. In Cairo today there are foreign-cuisine restaurants and American fast-food branches. On special occasions, middle-class Egyptians might dine in a restaurant that serves a foreign cuisine, but most Egyptians generally prefer their own food.

RELIGIOUS INFLUENCE

Religion has had a big influence on Egyptian eating habits. Most Egyptians, being Muslim, do not eat pork, and meat has to be slaughtered in a special ritual. A Muslim who knows how to kill the animal according to Islamic law cuts the windpipe of the animal while invoking the name of God, acknowledging Him as the creator of all things. The meat is then considered *halal*, or fit to eat.

Alcohol is forbidden under Islamic law; no Muslim should drink alcohol or sell it even to a non-Muslim. However, Egypt does have a large brewing industry, and most restaurants list beer on their drink menu. Beer is also offered to guests at weddings and other family feasts. People are far stricter on the alcohol rule during Ramadan, when restaurants and hotels usually sell alcoholic beverages only to tourists.

MEAT

Egyptians eat mostly lamb and mutton. Beef is not as common, as the land is not suitable for raising cattle. Roasted pigeon is a delicacy in the Egyptian countryside; many rural households keep an elaborate dovecote, and when there is a feast a pigeon is roasted and served as the main course. Camel and water buffalo meat is popular in the poorer homes.

Egypt's traditional source of seafood is the Mediterranean coast, but with modern modes of transportation the Red Sea has become another important source.

Fish for sale. Flanked by the Mediterranean and Red seas, Egypt has an abundance of seafood.

Egyptians have many cakes and pastries to satisfy their sweet tooth.

A SWEET TOOTH

Egyptians like sweet foods. They may have their pastries and cakes after meals or with tea or coffee between mealtimes.

Halvah and baklava are popular in Egypt and in many other Middle Eastern and Mediterranean countries as well. Baklava are small pastries made from paper-thin sheets of dough, filled with nuts, and sweetened with honey. Halvah are similar, but are made from semolina, or rice flour.

There are many variations of halvah and baklava; the differences lie mostly in the filling. Some of the pastries may be filled with dried fruit, such as dates, figs, or apricots, while others are filled or decorated with ground nuts, such as pistachios or walnuts. Baklava may be dipped in syrup or honey. The flavor of each sweet is identified by its shape.

Halvah and baklava are sold in cake shops in most towns in Egypt. Large bakeries display 20 or more kinds of halva and baklava that go by delightful names such as "lady's wrist" and "eat and promise." Bakers work nonstop to refill the trays as orders roll in.

Another popular Egyptian dessert is *bassboussa* (bas-BOO-sah), a cake made from yogurt, semolina, milk, and butter, baked until golden brown, and then covered with syrup.

DRINKS

Egyptians drink a lot of tea and coffee. They like strong tea, and drink it with milk in the morning and plain the rest of the day. Teas spiced with jasmine, rose, mint, or saffron are popular. Fresh sugarcane juice is a refreshing thirst quencher, and hibiscus leaves are used to make a drink called *karkadeh* (kahr-KAH-deh).

Customers at an Egyptian café enjoy a friendly game of dominoes and a smoke after drinking coffee and tea.

Coffee is the national drink. Egyptians drink coffee after meals, when they visit people's homes during the day, and at cafés after work.

There are two ways of serving coffee in Egypt: the Arab way and the Turkish way. Both kinds of coffee are made from green beans roasted brown, and both are served black in small cups.

The difference between the two lies in how they are made. Turkish coffee is boiled in a pot that narrows from the bottom to the top, which intensifies the foaming action during the boiling. The water, coffee, and sugar are mixed according to the individual's preference, and the pot is taken off the fire as soon as the coffee boils. It is put back on at least once to build up a foaming head. Then the coffee is poured into a small cup along with the coffee grounds, which settle at the bottom of the cup.

Arab coffee is prepared in a single boil. Sugar is seldom added, and spices such as cloves or cardamom may be added for flavor. Once the coffee boils, it is poured into a second pot without the grounds.

STREET FOOD

Virtually every street corner in Egypt has a stall selling food. Each day millions of people in the big cities will stop on the street to purchase a quick but filling snack.

Street stalls are particularly busy at breakfast time. The most popular breakfast is a round, flat bread that has been split open and filled with a spoonful of *foul* flavored with olive oil and lemon juice. This makes a fast and cheap meal, costing the equivalent of a few cents. Beans are known as "poor man's meat" in Egypt, but *foul* is an equally popular breakfast for rich Egyptians.

Falafel is another favorite street food. It is made from ground chick peas with green vegetables mixed with spices and deepfried. Falafel can be eaten on its own or placed inside a pita bread.

Other street vendors sell fried eggplant, stuffed peppers, or baked sweet potatoes. In the villages, or in the neighborhoods in Cairo, the vendors usually operate late into the night, their stalls lit by kerosene lamps. Some stall owners may even provide chairs for their customers.

Another popular food that people buy on the street is *shawarma*. This is usually sold from the front of small shops, as more equipment is needed for the preparation of this food. Marinated lamb or chicken slices are stacked one on top of another on a *shawarma* machine, which consists of a vertical skewer rotating over a charcoal fire. As the skewer rotates, the outer parts of the meat cook first. When a customer comes, the chef slices the meat on the outside and puts the slices into a split round of bread.

Egyptians from all walks of life patronize street stalls from morning to night.

128

BREAD

Bread forms a central part of the Egyptian diet; people eat it at virtually every meal. Even at a big dinner, there will still be a plate full of bread. It has been estimated that many Egyptians eat as much as 3 pounds (1.4 kg) of bread a day.

Egyptian bread is round and flat, and about the size of a small dinner plate. The bread is hollow and can be split down the middle for cooked meats or vegetables to be put inside.

Egyptians eat so much bread that the country has to import wheat to supplement wheat crops grown domestically. Since it is such a big part of the people's diet, the government subsidizes the cost of bread so that a few cents will buy an armful.

However, the subsidy is a heavy burden on the country's financial resources, and when the government tried to raise bread prices in 1977, riots broke out in Cairo. The government has since allowed only token increases in the price of bread.

KOUSHARI

This main course of lentils, macaroni, and rice is a typical Egyptian dish, cooked by rich and poor alike. This recipe serves eight.

3 large onions, sliced
4 cups water
Oil for frying
2 cups rice
2 teaspoons salt
1½ cups brown lentils, washed

8 ounces (227 g) elbow macaroni
6 cloves garlic, sliced
2 tablespoons white vinegar
6 ounces (170 g) tomato paste
2 teaspoons cumin
Chili pepper (optional)

Sauté the onions until brown, then drain on a paper towel. In a pot, boil 3 cups water with a few drops of oil. Carefully add the rice and 1 teaspoon salt, boil again, then simmer. Boil the lentils and the macaroni separately until tender, then drain away the water. Layer the rice, lentils, and macaroni in a serving dish. To make the sauce, sauté the garlic in a little oil, then add the vinegar, tomato paste, cumin, and remaining salt and water (and chili pepper, if desired). Boil the mixture, then simmer. To serve, spread the sauce over the rice, lentils, and macaroni in the serving dish, and garnish with the fried onions.

RIZ BI LABAN

This rice pudding is a simple but popular Egyptian dessert. This recipe serves eight.

³/₄ cup white rice
4¹/₄ cups milk
1 teaspoon vanilla extract
1 cup cold water
1¹/₄ cups sugar
Raisins
Almonds or pistachios

Rinse the rice several times, then set aside. Boil the milk over medium heat. Add the vanilla to the water, then add the water and the rice to the milk. Boil again over medium heat for half an hour, stirring constantly and gradually turning up the heat. Take the mixture off the fire and set aside for an hour. Return to low heat, and add more milk if desired. When the mixture has thickened, add the sugar and mix well. Continue boiling over low heat, until bubbles break through. Serve warm or cold in small bowls, and garnish with raisins and nuts.

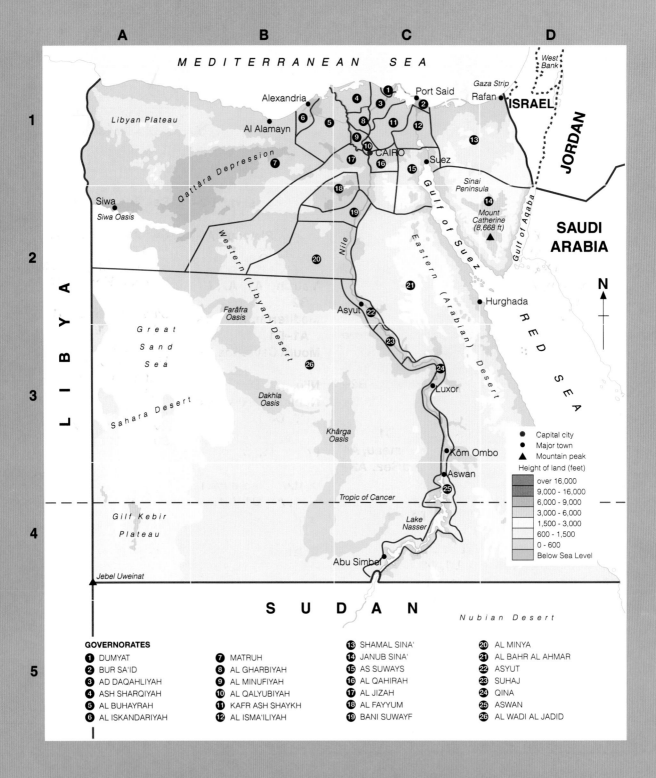

A B C D

MEDITERRANEAN SEA

West Bank

Gaza Strip

Alexandria
Port Said
Rafan
ISRAEL

Libyan Plateau

JORDAN

Al Alamayn

CAIRO
Suez

Qattâra Depression

Sinai Peninsula

SAUDI ARABIA

Siwa
Siwa Oasis

Mount Catherine (8,668 ft)

Gulf of Aqaba

Gulf of Suez

N

Western (Libyan) Desert

Nile

Eastern (Arabian) Desert

Hurghada

Farâfra Oasis

Great Sand Sea

Asyut

RED SEA

Dakhla Oasis

Sahara Desert

Khârga Oasis

Luxor

● Capital city
● Major town
▲ Mountain peak

Height of land (feet)

| over 16,000 |
| 9,000 - 16,000 |
| 6,000 - 9,000 |
| 3,000 - 6,000 |
| 1,500 - 3,000 |
| 600 - 1,500 |
| 0 - 600 |
| Below Sea Level |

Kôm Ombo

Aswan

Tropic of Cancer

Gilf Kebir Plateau

Lake Nasser

Jebel Uweinat

Abu Simbel

SUDAN

Nubian Desert

GOVERNORATES

① DUMYAT
② BUR SA'ID
③ AD DAQAHLIYAH
④ ASH SHARQIYAH
⑤ AL BUHAYRAH
⑥ AL ISKANDARIYAH

⑦ MATRUH
⑧ AL GHARBIYAH
⑨ AL MINUFIYAH
⑩ AL QALYUBIYAH
⑪ KAFR ASH SHAYKH
⑫ AL ISMA'ILIYAH

⑬ SHAMAL SINA'
⑭ JANUB SINA'
⑮ AS SUWAYS
⑯ AL QAHIRAH
⑰ AL JIZAH
⑱ AL FAYYUM
⑲ BANI SUWAYF

⑳ AL MINYA
㉑ AL BAHR AL AHMAR
㉒ ASYUT
㉓ SUHAJ
㉔ QINA
㉕ ASWAN
㉖ AL WADI AL JADID

LIBYA

MAP OF EGYPT

ECONOMIC EGYPT

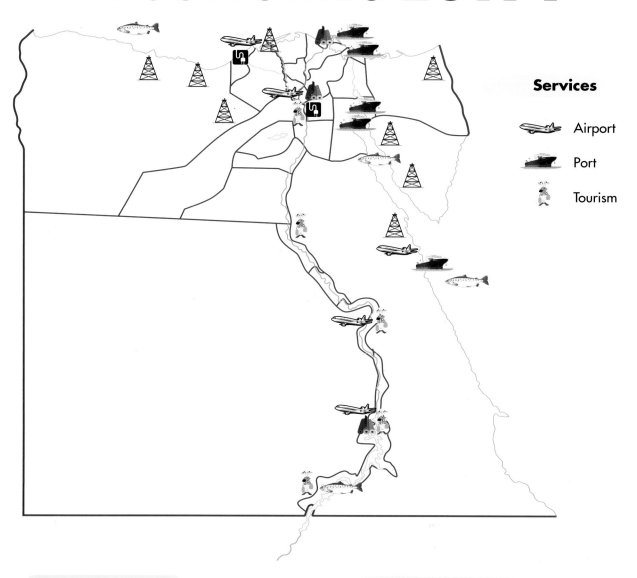

Services

 Airport

Port

 Tourism

Natural Resources

 Fish

 Oil/Natural Gas

Manufacturing

Electronics

Textiles

ABOUT
THE ECONOMY

OVERVIEW
Since the 1990s, Egypt has implemented reforms to reduce inflation and attract foreign investment. However, infrastructural spending and fluctuating tourism and export revenues have put pressure on the economy. In addition to its oil industry, Egypt is also developing its natural gas potential.

GROSS DOMESTIC PRODUCT (GDP)
US$258 billion (2001 estimate)

GDP SECTORS
Agriculture 14 percent, industry 30 percent, services 56 percent

NATURAL RESOURCES
Crude oil, natural gas, asbestos, gypsum, limestone, iron ore, lead, zinc

LAND AREA
384,345 square miles (995,450 square km)

AGRICULTURAL PRODUCTS
Beans, corn, cotton, fruit, rice, vegetables, wheat

CURRENCY
1 Egyptian pound (EGP) = 100 piasters
Notes: 1, 5, 10, 20, 50, 100 pounds; 25, 50 piasters
Coins: 5, 10, 25 piasters
USD 1 = EGP 5.90 (May 2003)

INFLATION RATE
2.3 percent (2001 estimate)

LABOR FORCE
20.6 million (2001 estimate)

LABOR FORCE BY OCCUPATION
Agriculture 29 percent, industry 22 percent, services 49 percent

UNEMPLOYMENT RATE
12 percent (2001 estimate)

AGRICULTURAL PRODUCTS
Beans, corn, cotton, fruit, rice, vegetables, wheat

INDUSTRIAL PRODUCTS
Cement, chemicals, food products, metal products, petroleum products, textiles

MAJOR EXPORTS
Chemicals, cotton, crude oil, metal products, petroleum products, textiles

MAJOR IMPORTS
Chemicals, fuels, machinery, wood products, food products

MAJOR TRADE PARTNERS
United States, Italy, Germany, countries in Asia and the Middle East

MAJOR PORTS
Alexandria, Aswan, Asyut, Damietta, Matruh, Port Said, Suez

CULTURAL EGYPT

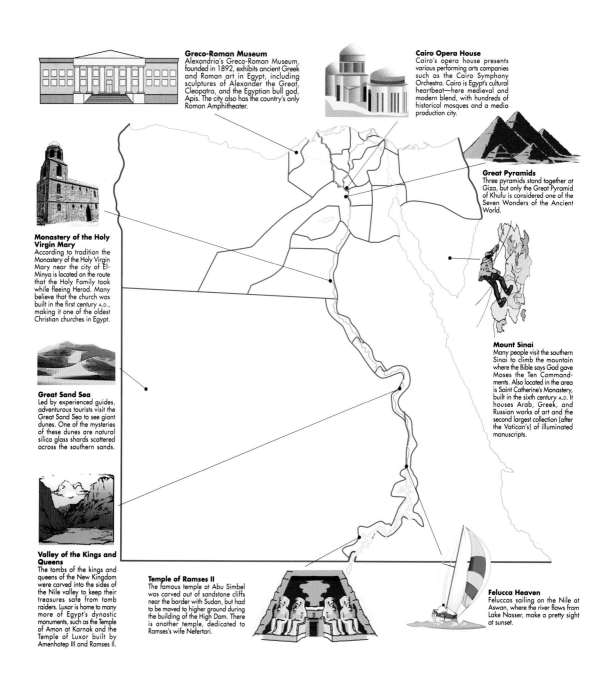

Greco-Roman Museum
Alexandria's Greco-Roman Museum, founded in 1892, exhibits ancient Greek and Roman art in Egypt, including sculptures of Alexander the Great, Cleopatra, and the Egyptian bull god, Apis. The city also has the country's only Roman Amphitheater.

Cairo Opera House
Cairo's opera house presents various performing arts companies such as the Cairo Symphony Orchestra. Cairo is Egypt's cultural heartbeat—here medieval and modern blend, with hundreds of historical mosques and a media production city.

Great Pyramids
Three pyramids stand together at Giza, but only the Great Pyramid of Khufu is considered one of the Seven Wonders of the Ancient World.

Monastery of the Holy Virgin Mary
According to tradition the Monastery of the Holy Virgin Mary near the city of El-Minya is located on the route that the Holy Family took while fleeing Herod. Many believe that the church was built in the first century A.D., making it one of the oldest Christian churches in Egypt.

Mount Sinai
Many people visit the southern Sinai to climb the mountain where the Bible says God gave Moses the Ten Commandments. Also located in the area is Saint Catherine's Monastery, built in the sixth century A.D. It houses Arab, Greek, and Russian works of art and the second largest collection (after the Vatican's) of illuminated manuscripts.

Great Sand Sea
Led by experienced guides, adventurous tourists visit the Great Sand Sea to see giant dunes. One of the mysteries of these dunes are natural silica glass shards scattered across the southern sands.

Valley of the Kings and Queens
The tombs of the kings and queens of the New Kingdom were carved into the sides of the Nile valley to keep their treasures safe from tomb raiders. Luxor is home to many more of Egypt's dynastic monuments, such as the Temple of Amon at Karnak and the Temple of Luxor built by Amenhotep III and Ramses II.

Temple of Ramses II
The famous temple at Abu Simbel was carved out of sandstone cliffs near the border with Sudan, but had to be moved to higher ground during the building of the High Dam. There is another temple, dedicated to Ramses's wife Nefertari.

Felucca Heaven
Feluccas sailing on the Nile at Aswan, where the river flows from Lake Nasser, make a pretty sight at sunset.

ABOUT THE CULTURE

OFFICIAL NAME
Arab Republic of Egypt

CAPITAL
Cairo

OTHER MAJOR CITIES
Al Mansura, Alexandria, Aswan, Asyut, Beni Suwaif, Damietta, Isma'ilia, Luxor, Port Said, Suez, Tanta

GOVERNMENT
A republic, with a president and a prime minister supported by a cabinet of ministers, a bicameral legislature, and a judiciary.

NATIONAL FLAG
The red band represents the pre-revolution era, the white band the advent of the revolution, and the black band the end of British occupation. The national emblem, in the middle band, consists of a shield on the breast of an eagle above a scroll with Egypt's Arabic name.

NATIONAL ANTHEM
Lyrics and music by Sayed Darwish. (To listen, go to www.sis.gov.eg/anthem/html/anthem.htm.)

POPULATION
70,712,345 (2002)

LIFE EXPECTANCY
64 years (2002)

AGE STRUCTURE
14 years and below: 34 percent; 15 to 64 years: 62 percent; 65 years and over: 4 percent (2002)

LANGUAGES
Arabic (official), English, French

LITERACY RATE
55 percent (2000)

INTERNET USERS
600,000 (2002)

ETHNIC GROUPS
Hamitic Arab, Bedouin, and Amazigh 99 percent; Nubian, European, and other 1 percent

RELIGIOUS GROUPS
Muslim 94 percent, Christian and other 6 percent

HOLIDAYS
Christmas (January 7), Eid al-Fitr and Eid al-Adha (dates vary), Muharram (March 5), Sinai Liberation Day (April 25), Sham el-Nessim (April 28), Labor Day (May 1), Mouled al-Nabi (May 13), Revolution Day (July 23), Armed Forces Day (October 6)

LEADERS IN POLITICS
Gamal Abdel Nasser—first president (1956–70)
Anwar al-Sadat—first Arab leader to visit Israel; 1978 Nobel Peace Prize winner
Hosni Mubarak—current president (since 1981)

TIME LINE

IN EGYPT	IN THE WORLD
5th millennium B.C. First settlers in the Nile delta	
2925 B.C. First pharaonic dynasty is established.	
2780 B.C. First pyramid is built for King Djoser.	**753 B.C.** Rome is founded.
332 B.C. Alexander the Great invades Egypt.	**116–17 B.C.** Roman empire reaches its greatest extent, under Emperor Trajan (98-17).
51–30 B.C. Reign of Cleopatra VII, the last pharaoh	
A.D. 395 Start of Byzantine rule	**A.D. 600** Height of Mayan civilization
639 Arabs introduce Islam.	
973 Fatimids establish Cairo as the capital.	**1000** Chinese perfect gunpowder and begin to use it in warfare.
1250 Mamluk rule begins.	
1517 Egypt becomes part of the Ottoman empire.	**1530** Beginning of trans-Atlantic slave trade organized by the Portuguese in Africa.
	1558–1603 Reign of Elizabeth I of England
	1620 Pilgrims sail the *Mayflower* to America.
	1776 U.S. Declaration of Independence
	1789–1799 French Revolution
1798 Napoleon Bonaparte invades Egypt.	
	1861 U.S. Civil War begins.
1869 Suez Canal is opened.	

IN EGYPT	IN THE WORLD
1882	
British begin to colonize Egypt.	
	1914
	World War I begins.
1936	**1939**
Farouk I becomes king.	World War II begins.
	1945
	United States drops atomic bombs on Hiroshima and Nagasaki.
	1949
1952	North Atlantic Treaty Organization (NATO) is formed.
Revolution turns Egypt into a republic.	
1956	
Gamal Abdel Nasser becomes president.	**1957**
	Russians launch Sputnik.
	1966–1969
1967	Chinese Cultural Revolution
Israeli troops take the Sinai.	
1970	
President Nasser dies; Anwar al-Sadat becomes president.	
1977	
President Sadat visits Jerusalem.	
1979	
Egypt and Israel sign a peace treaty; Israeli troops withdraw from the Sinai.	
1981	
President Sadat is assassinated; Hosni Mubarak becomes president.	**1986**
	Nuclear power disaster at Chernobyl in Ukraine
1989	
Egypt rejoins the Arab League.	
1991	**1991**
Egypt joins the international alliance to expel Iraq from Kuwait.	Break-up of the Soviet Union
1997	**1997**
President Mubarak launches the 20-year Toshka construction project.	Hong Kong is returned to China.
	2003
	War in Iraq.

GLOSSARY

fellahin
Peasants.

felucca
A long, narrow vessel propelled by oars or sails or both.

galabia (GEH-lah-bia)
An ankle-length outfit with long sleeves worn by men in the countryside.

hajj
The pilgrimage to Mecca.

ihram (EE-rahm)
White clothing worn by male pilgrims while performing the hajj.

imam
The religious or prayer leader at a mosque.

Ka'bah (KAH-AH-bah)
The central shrine of Islam located in the center of the Grand Mosque in Mecca; the focal point for daily prayer and the hajj.

khedive (kai-DEV)
The name given to the Turkish governor of Egypt from 1867 to 1914.

mahr (MAHR)
Money that the groom gives to the bride's father.

mazoun (MAA-zoon)
A government witness at a wedding.

muezzin
The mosque official who makes the prayer call.

oasis
A fertile spot in the desert watered by a spring, stream, or well.

papyrus
A water reed, common in ancient Egypt, used for making paper.

sakiya (se-KAY-ya)
An ancient irrigation method that uses a vertical waterwheel with buckets attached.

shadoof (shah-DOOF)
An ancient irrigation method that uses a bucket, a long pole, and large stones.

shariah (SHA-ri-ah)
Islamic law.

Sunni
One of two major divisions in Islam (the other is Shi'a). Sunni Muslims make up about 85 percent of the world's Muslims.

surah (SOO-rah)
A chapter of the Koran.

To Bedawi (TOW BAY-dah-wee)
A language spoken in the Eastern Desert.

wadi (wah-DEE)
An ancient desert valley that was once a riverbed.

FURTHER INFORMATION

BOOKS

Abdennour, Samia. *Egyptian Cooking: A Practical Guide*. New York: Hippocrene Books, 1998.

Al Misri, Mathaf and Araldo de Luca (photographer). *Egyptian Treasures from the Egyptian Museum in Cairo*. New York: Harry N. Abrams, 1999.

Collier, Mark and Bill Manley. *How to Read Egyptian Hieroglyphs: A Step-By-Step Guide to Teach Yourself*. Berkeley: University of California Press, 1998.

De Beler, Aude Gros and Aly Maher El Sayed. *The Nile*. Chicago: Independent Publishers Group, 2000.

Jenkins, Siona. *Lonely Planet Egyptian Arabic Phrasebook*. 2nd ed. California: Lonely Planet, 2001.

Macaulay, David. *Pyramid*. New York: Houghton Mifflin, 1982.

Mahfouz, Naguib. *The Cairo Trilogy: Palace Walk, Palace of Desire, Sugar Street*. London: Everyman's Library, 2001.

Parkinson, Richard and Stephen Quirke. *Papyrus*. Austin: University of Texas Press, 1995.

Tyldesley, Joyce. *Ramesses: Egypt's Greatest Pharaoh*. New York: Penguin USA, 2001.

Wise, Hilary. *Arabic at a Glance: Phrase Book and Dictionary for Travelers*. 2nd ed. New York: Barron's Educational Series, 2001.

WEBSITES

Ancient Egypt. www.ancientegypt.co.uk

Central Intelligence Agency World Factbook (select Egypt from the country list). www.cia.gov/cia/publications/factbook

Egypt State Information Service. www.sis.gov.eg

The Egyptian People's Assembly. www.assembly.gov.eg

The Egyptian Presidency. www.presidency.gov.eg

The Egyptian Shoura Assembly. www.shoura.gov.eg

Guardian's Egypt. www.guardians.net/egypt

Little Horus. www.horus.ics.org.eg

Lonely Planet World Guide: Destination Egypt. www.lonelyplanet.com/destinations/africa/egypt

Ministry of State for Environmental Affairs. www.eeaa.gov.eg

Tour Egypt: The Complete Guide to Ancient and Modern Egypt. www.touregypt.net

The World Bank Group (type "Egypt" in the search box). www.worldbank.org

World Travel Guide: Egypt. www.travel-guide.com/data/egy/egy.asp

VIDEOS

Egypt: Secrets of the Pharaohs. National Geographic, 1998. (VHS)

Egypt's Golden Empire. Warner Home Video, 2002. (DVD)

BIBLIOGRAPHY

Baines, John et al. *Religion in Ancient Egypt: Gods, Myths, and Personal Practice*. Ithaca: Cornell University Press, 1991.

Diamond, Arthur. *Egypt, Gift of the Nile*. New York: Dillon Press, 1992.

El Mahdy, Christine. *Mummies, Myth and Magic in Ancient Egypt*. New York: Thames and Hudson, 1989.

Hopwood, Derek. *Egypt: Politics and Society, 1945–1990*. London: Harper Collins Academic, 1991.

Murphy, Caryle. *Passion for Islam: Shaping the Modern Middle East: The Egyptian Experience*. Scribner, 2002.

Okijk, Pamela. *The Egyptians*. Columbus: Silver Burdett Press, 1989.

Shaw, Ian. *The Oxford History of Ancient Egypt*. Oxford: Oxford University Press, 2000.

Silverman, David P. *Ancient Egypt*. Oxford: Oxford University Press, 1997.

INDEX